11/9/89

To Warren

I always enjoy working
with you. Hope you enjoy the book.

ASSET ALLOCATION:
BALANCING
FINANCIAL RISK

ASSET ALLOCATION:
BALANCING
FINANCIAL RISK

Roger C. Gibson

Dow Jones-Irwin, Inc.
Homewood, Illinois 60430

This publication is designed to provide accurate and authoritative information in regard to the subject matter covered. It is sold with the understanding that the publisher is not engaged in rendering legal, accounting, or other professional service. If legal advice or other expert assistance is required, the services of a competent professional person should be sought.

From a Declaration of Principles jointly adopted by a Committee of the American Bar Association and a Committee of Publishers.

Project editor: Jean Roberts
Production manager: Carma W. Fazio
Jacket design: Image House
Production services: Editing, Design & Production, Inc.
Compositor: McFarland Graphics and Design Inc.
Typeface: 11/13 Century Schoolbook
Printer: The Maple-Vail Book Manufacturing Group

Library of Congress Cataloging-in-Publication Data

Gibson, Roger C.
    Asset allocation : balancing financial risk / Roger C. Gibson.
      p.   cm.
    Includes index.
    ISBN 1-55623-164-4
    1. Portfolio management. I. Title.
HG4529.5.G53   1990
332.6—dc20   89-34805
                                                            CIP

Printed in the United States of America
1 2 3 4 5 6 7 8 9 0 MP 6 5 4 3 2 1 0 9

This book is dedicated to Sarah and Adam.
You are the best kids a dad ever had!

The royalties from this book will be donated to the Roger C. Gibson Family Foundation in honor of my parents, Don B. and Marianne A. Gibson. The Foundation grants financial assistance to various charities for the alleviation of human suffering and supports educational and artistic endeavors.

ACKNOWLEDGMENTS

When this book was first conceived, a colleague of mine, Philip M. Gallagher, encouraged me to contact a top financial publisher, Dow Jones-Irwin. From the "speaking circuit," I had become friends with Michael D. Hirsch, author of *Multifund Investing.* He introduced me to his editor at Dow Jones-Irwin, who reviewed the outline for the book; and with his endorsement my publisher, Richard J. Borto, agreed to take on the project. Mr. Richard Staron, Editor-in-Chief of Dow Jones-Irwin, patiently stretched deadlines and guided the manuscript through the editing process to completion. Thanks to these gentlemen, I knew at the outset that the book would become a reality.

I am very grateful to Darwin M. Bayston, Executive Vice President of The Institute of Chartered Financial Analysts, who critiqued the first draft and made many helpful suggestions for improving the text. His enthusiasm lightened the burden of writing the final draft.

A book such as this is impossible without the assistance of many companies who graciously provided research support and capital market performance data. Accordingly, I would like to thank Ibbotson Associates, Inc.; Salomon Brothers, Inc.; Morgan Stanley Capital International Perspective;

A grammatical footnote:
    For grammatical clarity and consistency, the pronouns *he, his,* and *him* are used throughout the text rather than "he or she"; "his or her"; and "him or her." No sexual bias or insensitivity is intended.

Frank Russell Trust Company; National Council of Real Estate Investment Fiduciaries; National Association of Real Estate Investment Trusts, Inc.; Interfinancial Corporation; Trinity Investment Management Corporation; First Chicago Investment Advisors; CDA Investment Technologies, Inc.; and Vestek Systems, Inc.

My thanks to A. Gregory Lintner of Yanni•Bilkey Investment Consulting, Inc. who capably performed the computer work that produced many of the charts and graphs which summarize investment performance relationships. His associate, Keith R. Goldner, was also very helpful in formatting the charts and graphs.

I am grateful to Mary K. Ellison who corrected grammatical errors in the manuscript and reworded many sentences to give them greater clarity. From a combination of dictation and poor handwriting, my loyal assistant, Laraine C. Schmitt, tirelessly wordprocessed each draft of every page. She also coordinated the collection of research information and statistical data from the many organizations acknowledged above. Thanks, Laraine. I also want to thank the staff of Allegheny Financial Group, Ltd. who graciously consented to the use of their computer terminals and to Deborah J. Stahl who ran dozens of computer portfolio optimizations using Vestek software. Many of these optimizations are used in the book.

This is a book of concepts. Some are original, but many are borrowed. If you are intrigued by a certain idea, you will want to know the source. Where possible, I have acknowledged the author. Unfortunately, much of what is in my mind no longer has an identifiable origin. In these situations, I ask forgiveness from those who have shaped my thinking but who are not directly given credit. I also want to deliver from blame those whose ideas may have been altered based on my own perception and experience.

I especially want to thank Sir John M. Templeton who has been an inspiration to me both spiritually and professionally. I am very honored to have the Foreword to this book written by the man responsible for producing the world's best long-term investment track record. Such investment genius is exceedingly rare.

My thanks to the many investment and financial advisory professionals from across the country who have attended the presentations on asset allocation that I have been privileged to make at numerous conferences. The quality of dialogue at these meetings has been of great value in synthesizing the ideas in this book.

Finally, I would like to acknowledge and thank all of my clients, present and future, who make my profession as a money manager a challenging and rewarding experience.

Roger C. Gibson, CFA, CFP

FOREWORD

After 49 years of professional investment counseling world-wide, I believe that successful investing is mainly common sense. It is common sense to search for an asset where you can buy the greatest value for each dollar you pay. This means bargain hunting. For example, it is wise to compare a multitude of similar investments in order to select that one which can be bought for the lowest price in relation to other similar assets. If you buy a share of a company for a small fraction of its intrinsic value, then there is less risk of a major price decline and more opportunity for a major price increase.

To diversify your investments is clearly common sense so that those which produce more profits than expected will offset those which produce less. Even the best investment professional must expect that no more than two thirds of his decisions will prove to be above average in profits. Therefore, asset allocation and diversification are the foundation stones of successful long-term investing.

To diversify means that you do not put all of your assets in any one type of investment. Similarly, it is not wise to invest only in the shares of any one company, industry, or nation. If you search in all nations you are likely to find more good bargains and perhaps better bargains. Clearly you will reduce the risk because bear markets and business recessions occur at different times in different nations. Changing economic conditions also affect various types of investment assets differently. By diversifying among different types of assets, the value of your portfolio will not fluctuate as much.

To begin with modest assets and build a fortune obviously requires thrift. An investor seeking to become wealthy should adhere to an annual family expense budget that includes a large amount of savings. For example, during my first 15 years after college, I made a game of adhering to a budget that included saving 50 cents out of every dollar of earnings. Those who are thrifty will grow wealthy, and those who are spendthrift will become poor.

Also, there is a magic formula called *dollar-cost averaging* in which you invest the same amount of money at regular intervals in an investment whose price fluctuates. At the end of the investment period, your average cost will be below the average price paid for the investment. In other words, your dollars will buy more shares when prices are low and fewer shares when prices are high, so that your average cost is low compared with the average for the market.

John D. Rockefeller said that to grow wealthy you must have your money work for you. In other words, be a lender and not a borrower. For example, if you have a big mortgage on your home, the interest paid will more than double the cost of the home. On the other hand, if you own a mortgage on a house, the annual interest on that mortgage will compound and make a fortune for you. If you never borrow money, interest will always work for you and not against you. You will also have peace of mind and be able to live through the bear markets and business recessions that occur in most nations about twice every 10 years.

It is only common sense to prepare for a bear market. Experts do not know when each bear market will begin, but you can be certain that there will be many bear markets during your lifetime. Common sense investing means that you should prepare yourself both financially and psychologically. Financially you should be prepared to live through any bear market without having to sell at the wrong time. In fact, your financial planning should provide for additional investment funds so that you can buy when shares are unreasonably low in price. Preparing psychologically means to expect that there will be many bull markets and bear markets so that you will not sell at the wrong time or buy at the wrong time. To buy low and sell high is difficult for persons who are not psychologically prepared or who act on emotions rather than facts.

When my investment counsel company began in 1940, on the front page of our descriptive booklet were these words: "To buy when others are despondently selling and to sell when others are avidly buying requires the greatest fortitude and pays the greatest reward."

Probably no investment fact is more difficult to learn than the fact that the price of shares is never low except when most people are selling and never high except when most are buying. This makes investing totally different from other professions. For example, if you go to 10 doctors all of whom agree on the proper medicine, then clearly you should take that medicine. But if you go to 10 security analysts all of whom agree that you should buy a particular share or type of asset then quite clearly you must do the opposite. The reason is that if 100 percent are buying and then even one changes his mind and begins selling, then already you will have passed the peak price. Common sense is not common; but common sense and careful logic show that it is impossible to produce superior investment performance if you buy the same assets at the same time as others are buying.

When selecting shares for purchase there are many dozens of yardsticks for judging value. A most reliable yardstick is how high is the price in relation to earnings. However, it is even more important to ask how high is the price in relation to probable earnings 5 to 10 years in the future. A share is nothing more than a right to receive a share of future earnings. Growth in earnings usually results from superior management. Even the best professionals have great difficulty in judging the ability of management. For the part-time investor, the best way is to ask three questions. Is this company growing more rapidly than its competitors? Is the profit margin wider than its competitors? Are the annual earnings on invested assets larger than for competitors? These three simple indicators will tell you much about the ability of management.

History shows frequent and wide fluctuations in the prices of many types of assets. Proper asset allocation helps to dampen the impact that these price swings will have on your portfolio. Asset price fluctuations may be even greater and more frequent in the future because all human activity is speeding up. This is one reason why you should not select a professional adviser based on short-term performance. For example, an adviser who takes the most risk is likely to have top performance in a bull market and the opposite in a bear market. Individual investors as well as managers of pension funds and university endowments should judge the ability of investment advisers over at least one full market cycle and preferably several cycles. This helps to balance out the element of luck and reveal which adviser has received the blessing of common sense.

I hope that almost every adult will become an investor. When I became an investment counselor there were only 4 million shareholders in America, and now there are 48 million. The amount of money invested in American mutual funds is now 1,000 times as great as it was 55 years ago. Thrift, common sense, and wise asset allocation can produce excellent results in the long run. For example, if you begin at age 25 to invest 2,000 dollars annually into your Individual Retirement Account where it can compound free of tax, and if you average a total return of 10 percent annually, you will have nearly a million dollars accumulated at age 65.

Investment management requires the broad consideration of all major investment alternatives. In this book, Roger Gibson develops the principles of asset allocation which make for good common sense investing in a rapidly changing world. In easily understood terms, he guides investment advisers and their clients step-by-step through a logical process for making the important asset allocation decisions. The broadly diversified investment approach Roger Gibson advocates should give investment advisers and their clients good investment results with increased peace of mind.

John M. Templeton
Chairman of Templeton,
  Galbraith & Hansberger
April 11, 1989

CONTENTS

Let every man divide his money into three parts, and
invest a third in land, a third in business, and a third let
him keep in reserve.

—*Talmud*

INTRODUCTION

To know when one's self is interested, is the first
condition of interesting other people.
                              —*Walter Pater* (1839—1894)
                              Marius the Epicurean, 1885

I feel fortunate to be in the money management profession. The theory and practice of portfolio management have been a source of continual fascination and challenge. I enjoy working with my clients, and the professional opportunities are outstanding. The diversity of client situations, each with its own unique set of problems, fuels the search for new and better financial solutions. This keeps the student in me eager to continue learning. As I look back over my career, I can clearly see an evolution in my thought process which has gradually changed my money management approach. As my knowledge and understanding of the investment management process have changed, so has my notion of what constitutes an appropriate strategy in any given situation. The quality and value of my judgments are intimately tied to how accurately I evaluate the client's situation and how realistically I assess the likely outcomes of alternative strategies. As in medicine, if the condition is misdiagnosed, the prescribed treatment may be of little value to the patient.

The same principle is at work with respect to the quality of the client's investment decision-making process. When it comes to investments, everyone has an opinion and misconceptions abound. These misconceptions are most prevalent and dangerous in the area of asset allocation policy.

Often, this manifests itself in the form of a client's inappropriate rejection of a major investment asset category, much to the detriment of his portfolio. We all know, for example, of clients who refuse to invest in common stocks, or perhaps in bonds or real estate, even though the asset category may play an important part in developing the best strategy to reach their objectives. It is hardly surprising, therefore, that many clients have portfolios that accurately reflect their comfort levels and investment preferences, yet are completely inappropriate to their needs. In these situations it is not enough for the investment manager to clearly evaluate the client's circumstances and develop an appropriate strategy if the client does not have the conceptual knowledge and frame of reference to understand that the recommendations are in his best interest. Often an adviser and client agree to sidestep the problem by the client's abandonment of all aspects of the investment management process to the portfolio manager's discretion. In essence, the client says to the portfolio manager: "Investment management is your job, not mine. That's why I hired you. I trust you. Just tell me this time next year how we're doing." While trust is essential in a client-adviser relationship, it is generally not sufficient to carry the client through extreme market conditions when emotions are most likely to override reason.

The good news is that the problem has a solution. It involves educating the client regarding capital market behavior and the principles of investment portfolio management. With the proper frame of reference, an informed client can confidently assume his proper role in knowledgeably determining asset allocation policy with the guidance of the portfolio manager. Over time, the asset allocation decisions will be the primary determinants of a portfolio's risk/return characteristics. It is essential therefore that the client be actively involved.

This book presents a disciplined framework within which investment professionals and their clients can make the most important decisions impacting portfolio performance. A major theme is that successful money management requires successful management of the client's expectations. At the outset, it is acknowledged that for this decision-making framework to be successful in practice it must:

1. Be conceptually sound.
2. Be comprehensible to clients without requiring an inordinate time commitment on their part.
3. Facilitate the development of appropriate individually tailored solutions based on the client's unique needs and circumstances.
4. Be standardized with respect to the steps to be followed.
5. Continue to have relevance and effectiveness in the future throughout changing investment markets.

I will draw on and explore the concepts of modern portfolio theory as advisable for the purpose of enhancing the conceptual understanding of the subject matter. But my emphasis will be on the practical implications of these theories. Effectiveness in both managing money and working with clients is increased as the gap between theory and practice narrows. It is my hope that this book contributes to the development of better designed portfolios for clients—so that with higher confidence, clients will remain committed to the path that moves them toward the realization of their financial objectives.

CHAPTER 1

THE IMPORTANCE
OF ASSET ALLOCATION

Not only is there but one way of *doing* things rightly,
but there is only one way of *seeing* them, and that
is *seeing* the whole of them.

—John Ruskin (1819–1900)
The Two Paths, 1885

The capital markets have changed dramatically over the last few decades. Money management has undergone a concurrent evolution. In the early 1960s the term *asset allocation* did not exist. The traditional view of diversification was simply to "avoid putting all of your eggs in one basket." The argument was that if all of your money was placed in one investment, your range of possible outcomes was very wide—you might win very big, but you also had the possibility of losing very big. Alternatively, by spreading your money among a number of different investments, the likelihood was that you would not be either right on all of them or wrong on all of them at the same time. There was an advantage, therefore, in having a narrower range of outcomes.

For the individual investor those were the days when broad diversification meant owning several dozen stocks and bonds along with some cash equivalents. For large pension plans and other institutional portfolios, these same asset categories were often used in a balanced fund with a single manager. Because the United States' stock and bond markets constituted the major portion of the world capital markets, most investors did not even consider international investing. Bonds traded in a very narrow price range. Security analysis activity focused more on common stocks where the payoff seemed greatest for superior investment skill. The majority of transactions on capital market exchanges were noninstitutional, and so it was commonly believed that a full-time skilled professional should be able to "beat the market" consistently. The investment manager's job was to add value through successful market timing and/or superior security selection. The focus was much more on individual issues than it was on the total portfolio. The "prudent man rule," with its emphasis on individual assets, reinforced this type of thinking in the fiduciary community.

As time passed, bonds moved out of their narrow trading ranges as price volatility increased dramatically as a result of large swings in interest rates. A multimanager approach on both the debt and the equity portions of institutional portfolios replaced the single balanced manager. Institutional trading on the exchanges increased to more than 80 percent of all activity. The full-time professionals were no longer competing against amateurs, they were now competing against each other.

Imagine for a moment the floor of the New York Stock Exhange. Millions of transactions are occurring between willing buyers and sellers. Around any single transaction, the buyer has concluded that the security is worth more than the money, while the seller has concluded that the money is worth more than the security. Both parties to the transaction are likely to be institutions that have nearly instantaneous access to all publicly available relevant information concerning the value of the security. Each has very talented, well-educated investment analysts who have carefully evaluated this information and have interestingly reached opposite conclusions. At the moment of the trade, both parties are acting from a position of informed conviction, even though time will prove one of them right and the other one wrong. Because of the dynamics of a free market, their transaction price equates supply with demand for the security and thereby clears the market. A free market price is therefore a consensus of a security's intrinsic value. In the money management business the stakes are high and the rewards are correspondingly great for successful money managers who through skill are able to produce a consistently superior return. It is no wonder that so many bright, talented people are drawn to the profession. In such a marketplace, however, it is difficult to imagine that the market price for any widely followed security will depart meaningfully from its true underlying value. Such is the nature of an efficient market.

In both the money management and the academic communities there has been much ongoing controversy regarding the degree of efficiency of the capital markets. The debate has far-reaching implications. To the extent that a market is inefficient, opportunities exist for individuals to exercise superior skill to produce an above-average return. There do seem to be various "market anomalies" which indicate that the capital markets are not perfectly efficient. Most research evidence, however, supports the notion that the markets are reasonably efficient. The accelerating advances being made in information-processing technologies will undoubtedly drive the markets to become even more efficient in the future. It thus will become increasingly unlikely that anyone will be able to beat the market consistently.

The tremendous growth in the use of index funds serves as tangible evidence that the issue is not of academic curiosity alone. In an efficient marketplace the expectation is that active management with its associated transaction costs will result in below-average performance over time. If that is true, one way to win the game is never to play it at all. Those who have invested in index funds have chosen not to play the security selection game. It is ironic (yet logical) that the same high-powered money management talent that creates the efficiency of the marketplace makes the achievement of an above-average return so exceedingly difficult. Even in those rare situations where a money mangement organization has a unique proprietary insight that enables them to produce a superior result, the expectation is that the advantage will be eroded over time as other money management organizations discover and exploit the process.

Modern portfolio theory has as its foundation the notion of efficient capital markets. As this body of knowledge developed, the focus of attention shifted from individual securities to a consideration of the portfolio as a whole. There has been a simultaneous shift of attention away from return enhancement in favor of risk reduction through broad diversification. The interrelationships among securities within the portfolio are now considered to be as important as the risk/return characteristics of the individual securities. Modern portfolio theory redefined the notion of diversification. It went far beyond the idea of using a large number of baskets in which to carry one's eggs. Major emphasis must also be placed on finding baskets that are distinctly different from one another. That is important because each basket's unique pattern of returns partially offsets the others', with the effect of smoothing overall portfolio volatility.

Before modern portfolio theory, security analysis was a two-dimensional process focusing on the risk/return characteristics of individual securities. Modern portfolio theory added a third dimension to this process which evaluates a security's "diversification effect" on a portfolio. Diversification effect considers the impact that the inclusion of a particular asset category or security will have on the risk/return characteristics of the overall portfolio. In an efficient capital market, security prices are always fair. Given this, modern portfolio theory stresses that it is wise to simply "buy and hold" a broad array of diverse investments. These concepts were later given legislative endorsement in the Employee Retirement Income Security Act of 1974, which stressed the importance of diversification within a broad portfolio context.

The investment world of today is indeed very different from that of the past. The number and variety of investment alternatives have increased dramatically, and the once well-defined boundaries between asset categories often overlap one another. We now deal in a global marketplace in which the United States' share of the world capital markets has shrunk to a minority position. Computer technol-

ogy delivers relevant new information regarding a multitude
of investment alternatives almost instantaneously to a marketplace now dominated by institutional investors. The traditionally diversified domestic stock and bond portfolio is
clearly inadequate in today's investment environment.

Designing an investment portfolio consists of several
steps:

1. Deciding which asset categories will be represented
   in the portfolio.
2. Determining the long-term "target" percentage of the
   portfolio to allocate to each of these asset categories.
3. Specifying for each asset category the range within
   which the allocation can be altered in an attempt to
   exploit better performance possibilities from one asset
   category versus another.
4. Selection of securities within each of the asset categories.

The first two steps form the foundation for the portfolio's risk/return characteristics and are often referred to as
investment policy decisions. Traditionally, a diversified portfolio was built with three asset categories: cash equivalents,
bonds, and common stocks. Other asset categories, however,
should be explicitly considered. Among them, for example,
are international bonds, international common stocks, real
estate, and precious metals. To the extent to which these
various asset categories are affected differently by changing economic events, each will have its own unique pattern
of returns. It is the ability of one asset category's pattern of
returns to partially offset another asset category's pattern
that drives the power of diversification in reducing portfolio
risk. When considering which asset categories to include in
the portfolio, one should begin with the position that all major asset categories will be represented unless specific sound
reasons can be established for the exclusion of a particular
category or categories.

A variety of methods can be used for determining the
target weights assigned to each of the various asset categories. Modern portfolio theory suggests that in an efficient

market, an investor of average risk tolerance should hold a portfolio that mirrors the proportions in which the world's wealth is allocated among the various asset categories. This would give an asset allocation similar to that shown in Figure 1-1. In practice, however, clients vary considerably in their unique needs and circumstances. And the use of one target allocation for all clients is an example of "cutting the person to fit the cloth." The client's investment objective, relevant time horizon, and risk tolerance combine to determine whether his portfolio should be structured for greater principal stability with correspondingly lower returns, or alternatively for higher growth at the price of more volatility. In either case, the goal is to use the best allocation across the various asset categories in order to achieve the highest expected return relative to the risk assumed.

For step 3, minimum and maximum limits are often set for each asset category's portfolio commitment. If, for example, common stocks are judged to be unusually attrac-

FIGURE 1-1
Total Investable Capital Market as of December 31, 1988 (Preliminary) Note: May not add to 100% due to rounding

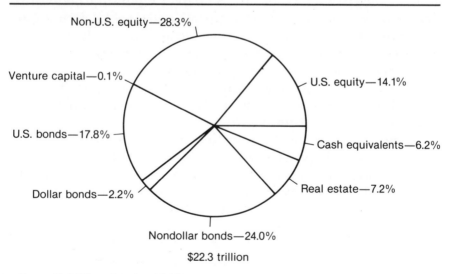

Non-U.S. equity—28.3%

Venture capital—0.1%

U.S. equity—14.1%

U.S. bonds—17.8%

Cash equivalents—6.2%

Dollar bonds—2.2%

Real estate—7.2%

Nondollar bonds—24.0%

$22.3 trillion

Source: First Chicago Investment Advisors.

tive relative to other asset categories, the allocation for common stocks is moved to its upper limit. At other times when common stocks appear to be overvalued, the commitment is moved down to its minimum allocation. This represents the "market timing" dimension of the investment management process. The success of market timing activities presumes the existence of inefficiencies in the pricing mechanism among asset categories, coupled with the superior skill needed to identify and act on that mispricing. In its most extreme form, market timing takes the form of allocating 100 percent of the portfolio to either cash equivalents or common stocks, in an attempt to participate fully in common stock bull markets while resting safely in cash equivalents during bear markets. The obvious danger of such an approach is in being in the wrong place at the wrong time with 100 percent of one's capital. The minimum and maximum limits set for each asset category in step 3 act to minimize this risk by requiring that the portfolio avoid extreme allocations.

Various strategies are used to attempt to identify and exploit asset category mispricing. Technical analysis, for example, attempts to predict future price movements on the basis of the patterns of past price movements and on the volume of security transactions. The overwhelming body of research evidence indicates that such approaches do not beat a naive buy and hold strategy. Other approaches rely on sophisticated forecasting procedures to determine the relative attractiveness of one asset category versus another. The same caveat exists with respect to the difficulty of seeing something everyone else is missing and being able to act confidently on that foresight.

For step 4, security selection can be accomplished actively or passively. If done passively, index funds can be used for the various asset categories in order to obtain the desired breadth of diversification while minimizing transaction costs and management fees. Active security selection is predicated on the belief that exploitable inefficiencies exist at the individual security level which can be identified through skilled analysis. To add value, an active manager must produce an incremental return in excess of the transaction costs and associated fees—a difficult although not necessarily impossible achievement in an efficient marketplace.

Traditionally, money management has been equated with steps 3 and 4 of the process—market timing and security selection. Ironically, it is because of the tremendous intelligence and skill of the investment professionals engaging in these activities that the probability for success in these areas is so low. Yet, the choice of asset categories and their respective weights in a portfolio has had, and will continue to have, a large impact on future performance. To many it is surprising that over time investment policy decisions regarding the choice of investment asset categories and their relative long-term weightings within the portfolio have a much greater impact on their portfolio's future investment performance than does the shifting of money among the asset categories and the selection of securities within asset categories.

The focus of "value added" is shifting decidedly in favor of a fuller involvement by both investment adviser and client with the issue of proper asset allocation. By definitively exploring these issues and committing the decisions to writing in the form of an investment policy statement, both investment adviser and client have the advantage of a common shared frame of reference for evaluating investment performance and monitoring progress being made relative to the achievement of objectives. Investment management is also demystified and the likelihood is increased that a properly conceived, sound investment strategy will be adhered to during those phases of the market cycle when the temptation to depart from established policy is at its height.

Dramatic support for the importance of asset allocation is provided by a study of 91 large pension plans covering the period 1974 through 1983.[1] The Brinson et al. study sought to attribute the variation of total returns among the plans to three factors: asset allocation, market timing, and security selection. The study concluded that on average a startling

---

[1]Gary P. Brinson, L. Randolph Hood, and Gilbert L. Beebower, "Determinants of Portfolio Performance," *Financial Analysts Journal*, July–August 1986, pp. 39–44.

93.6 percent of the variation could be explained by the asset allocation policy followed. Market timing, in conjunction with asset allocation policy, explained 95.3 percent of the variation in total returns among the plans. Similarly, 97.8 percent of the variation in total returns among the plans was explained by the combination of asset allocation with security selection. The study dramatically supports the notion that asset allocation policy is the primary determinant of investment performance, with market timing and security selection both playing a minor role.

If security selection and market timing have surprisingly little to do with determining long-term investment performance, why is so much attention obstinately focused in this area? Part of the reason is historical. The money management profession is rooted in the notion that superior skill can beat the market. Traditionally, investment management has been synonymous with market timing and security selection. Many investment professionals wrongly conclude that were it not for the expectation of superior results from these tasks, the profession would not exist.

The realities of the marketplace, however, stubbornly persist. Research studies repeatedly show that most money managers underperform the market on average over time, and those who do outperform the market in one time period do not have a better than even chance of outperforming the market in the next time period. This is not a surprising conclusion. The marketplace is populated by professionals and, by definition, the majority cannot outperform the average. Given the transaction costs and management fees incurred in attempting to do so, it is expected that in the future most money managers will continue to underperform the market as a whole. The hope offered through market timing and security selection has tremendous seductive appeal. All investors want to enjoy the pleasures of a good market and avoid the pain of a bad market. As a result, the hypothesis that most professional money managers can add value through successful market timing and security selection has never been challenged in the minds of many. As data emerges to refute the hypothesis, the tendency has often been to attempt a revision of the data to fit the hypothesis. The client's misconceptions and wishful thinking often support the process, given his desire to find money managers willing to assure him of superior results.

An example of revising the data to fit the hypothesis concerns screening the performance of money managers in an attempt to find those with superior skills. In an article in a recent issue of a popular financial magazine, several hundred mutual funds were reviewed. The author advised against making a judgment based on one year's superior results. Instead, he suggested finding managers who maintained above-average performance results in each of the past five years. The investor could then choose from among these "better" money managers. However, this approach does not adequately differentiate between above-average results produced by luck versus those produced by skill.

Consider, for example, a group of 1,000 money managers, each of whom makes security decisions on the basis of a random process, like rolling dice. At the end of the first year we can rank these 1,000 money managers on the basis of their returns. By definition, 500 will be above average, and 500 will be below average. Eliminating those with below-average performance in the first year, the remaining above-average managers continue rolling dice and making security selections through the second year. Half of these will be above average and half will be below average. Those who underperform will again be eliminated from consideration. Continuing in this manner, by the end of the fifth year, we will have a group of slightly more than 30 who had above-average performance in each of the five years. Our knowledge of the random process used by these managers to make security selections prevents us from attributing superior selection to the results achieved. In the real world of money management, however, where the promise of superior results is often made, identifying 30 managers out of a universe of 1,000 who have outperformed the market in each of the preceding five years can lead one to be too quick to assume that the performance is due to superior skill rather than luck.

Given the complexity of the investment management process, there will always be a wide dispersion of returns produced by various money managers during any particular time frame. This dispersion produces an illusion that the skill levels of these managers vary as much as do their results. In reality, short-run variations in performance are heavily influenced by chance. Without realizing this, many investors continue to compare their performance against the results achieved by the latest investment "guru." In the end, investors often chase those performance numbers by constantly reallocating money from one manager to another, as the search goes on for the elusive money manager who will produce the same superior performance tomorrow that was produced for someone else yesterday.

This does not imply that managers with superior skill do not exist, but rather that they are rare and extraordinarily difficult to conclusively identify. Professor Barr Rosenberg suggests a statistical approach to determine the length of time that above-average performance must continue in order for the appraiser to be confident that the incremental return is attributable to superior skill rather than to luck. This calculation indicates that very long periods of time are usually required—often several decades. By this yardstick, the impressive long-term track records of rare investment managers such as John M. Templeton and a handful of others attest to the impact that truly superior skill can have on investment results.

The expected payoff from superior skill will vary depending upon where the skill is directed. Not all sectors of the capital markets are equally efficient. For example, smaller capitalization companies do not command as much institutional research as large capitalization companies. Similarly, various foreign capital markets are probably not as efficient as the U.S. capital market. Where inefficiencies exist, there may be exploitable opportunities for superior investment analysis to produce value added. These opportunities should not be overlooked. But it should also be expected that, over time, the increasing efficiency of the market will continue to narrow the possible incremental rewards from superior skill as more investors act to exploit these opportunities.

For centuries, Sir Isaac Newton's conception of the laws of nature was accepted without question. The universe followed deterministic, billiard-ball-like laws of cause and effect. The work of Albert Einstein ended this world view. Modern physics has changed the notions of time and space. Now the universe is viewed in a context in which everything is relative to everything else. Einstein's work did not invalidate Newton's laws of physics. It merely defined the limited context within which Newton's mechanistic laws are true. Likewise, traditional money management with its emphasis on individual security selection, has been eclipsed by modern portfolio theory, which in the spirit of Einstein, considers each asset category not as an end in itself but rather as it stands in relationship to all others. Modern portfolio theory does not invalidate traditional money management approaches so much as it prescribes the limits within which they are valid and can add value. (Indeed, without financial analysis, and the buying and selling activities of intelligent investors, the marketplace would not be as efficient as it is!)

Money management today is being transformed within the wider and more important context of asset allocation and investment policy. The goal is no longer to beat the market, but rather to devise appropriate long-term strategies that will move clients to their objectives with the least amount of risk. These strategies do not fight the capital markets so much as they intelligently ride with them. Money management today requires an all-encompassing approach in its view of the investment world, as well as in its view of the client's situation. As investment advisers, we can be very valuable to our clients by first devising for them rational investment policies that will help them realize their objectives over time and then encouraging them to adhere to these policies. Our clients have been trained to look over our shoulders and evaluate our performance. If they *perceive* that our methods are not working, they will look for a new adviser. In investment management, perceptions often differ from reality. That is why it is so important that both the client and his adviser share a common frame of reference regarding the capital markets and the investment management process. It is easy to fall into the trap of presuming that clients have a grasp of basic investment concepts when in reality their understanding may be quite limited. At the risk of being rudimentary, it is advisable to avoid this danger by taking the time to define terms and explain concepts to clients at the outset. In the next chapter we will discuss the historical performance of the capital markets. Keep in mind that although the information may be familiar to you, it is unknown territory to many clients. For this reason, we shall engage in this review of the basics, in order to give you a methodology for developing a common frame of reference with your clients. Armed with knowledge, your clients will be more comfortable with the investment policies most appropriate for them.

CHAPTER 2

A HISTORICAL REVIEW OF CAPITAL MARKET INVESTMENT PERFORMANCE

Hindsight is always twenty-twenty.

—*Billy Wilder* (1906–   )
Columbo's Hollywood

Extensive questionnaires are often compiled during the initial meeting between a prospective client and a money manager. Clients are asked to describe the facts of their financial situation, state their investment objectives, and specify their risk tolerance. With this information, the money manager designs a suitable investment strategy. There are problems, however. What assurance does a money manager have that a client has realistic expectations regarding investment performance? Can the money manager be confident that the client clearly perceives all the risks involved in the money management process and the relative importance of those risks?

Often such problems are easily identified. An example would be a client who states, "I want to earn a compound annual return of between 15 percent and 25 percent, but I don't want to take any chances with my principal—I'm basically a conservative person." It is generally agreed that a successful investment strategy must be consistent with a client's risk tolerance. It is less obvious, however, that a client's stated tolerance for risk may be inordinately influenced by fears triggered by a lack of investment knowledge. Here the problem lies not within the capital markets but rather within the client.

An investment-advisory relationship will inevitably encounter difficulties if the client has a different "investment world view" than the adviser. This situation is a time bomb waiting to explode. In October 1987 the United States' stock market experienced the largest single-day decline in history. Following the crash, an advisory relationship would have been in trouble if the money manager's investment strategy was predicated on the notion that market timing is not possible, but the client believed that it was the money manager's job to protect him from stock market declines. Clients' expectations tend to err in optimistic directions. Generally, people believe that higher returns are possible with less risk than is actually the case. An important rule in investment management is therefore to first manage the client's expectations, then manage his money. It is critical that the client and money manager share a common investment world view before the investment strategy is implemented. Realistic expectations are needed for the development of realistic objectives. Clients must understand *all* types of risks and must accurately assess the relative importance of each type in their particular situations. The myth of the "ideal investment" must be destroyed. There are no liquid investment alternatives with stable guaranteed principal values which can provide real returns by consistently beating the combined impact of inflation and income taxes. Any misconceptions that go uncorrected will have a tendency to surface later, often to the detriment of the investment management process. Clients also need to be educated about the importance of *time horizon* in establishing an appropriate investment strategy. These educational tasks can be accomplished with a thorough review of the historical performance of the capital markets. The investment world view that emerges from this process serves as a foundation for the investment philosophy and money management approach used in helping clients to reach their objectives.

One of the best sources of up-to-date information regarding the investment performance of various investment alternatives is Ibbotson Associates' Yearbook, *Stocks, Bonds, Bills, and Inflation.* The data covers the time period 1926 to the present. During these decades, the capital markets experienced periods of both war and peace, inflation and deflation, and several cycles of economic expansion and contraction. Figure 2-1 traces the cumulative effect of compounded total returns on $1.00 invested at the end of 1925 for various

FIGURE 2-1
Wealth Indices of Investments in U.S. Capital Markets (1926–1988; Year-end 1925 = 1.00)

Source: Roger G. Ibbotson and Rex A. Sinquefield, *Stocks, Bonds, Bills, and Inflation* (SBBI), 1982, updated in *SBBI 1989 Yearbook,* Ibbotson Associates, Chicago.

investment alternatives. These performance figures are not adjusted for the impact of income taxes and generally do not take into consideration transaction costs. The vertical axis on the graph is a logarithmic scale, where a given vertical distance represents a specific percentage change, regardless of where it is measured. A logarithmic scale is often used to facilitate the comparison on the same graph of alternatives with widely varying results.

INFLATION

The measure of inflation used in Figure 2-2 is the Consumer Price Index (CPI) as compiled by the Bureau of Labor Statistics. Many experts prefer the Gross National Product Deflator as a better measurement of inflation, but the CPI is widely publicized and more commonly used. As a proxy for the cost of living, let us assume that at the end of 1925 a breakfast of bacon and eggs, toast, and coffee costs $1.00. During the following 63 years, inflation increased the cost of living approximately seven times, pushing the price of this same breakfast to $6.72 by the end of 1988. The first seven years of this period, however, were deflationary, averaging a compound decline in the cost of living of 4.4 percent per year, reducing the price of our hypothetical breakfast to $.73 by the end of 1932. It was not until the end of 1945 that inflation had pushed the cost of our breakfast back to $1.00. The nearly sevenfold increase in the cost of living shown in Figure 2-2 is therefore primarily a story of the inflation following World War II. Historically, wars often have been accompanied by periods of high inflation, but usually a postwar deflation would bring price levels back down again. This did not occur, however, following World War II. Inflation continued, although at a modest compound annual rate of 2.8 percent over the next two decades. From the mid-1960s through 1981 inflation became much more serious, compounding at an average rate of 7 percent annually. At this pace, the cost of living doubles approximately every decade. From 1982 through 1988 inflation returned to a more modest 3.6 percent compound annual rate.

FIGURE 2-2
Inflation: Rates of Change and Cumulative Indices

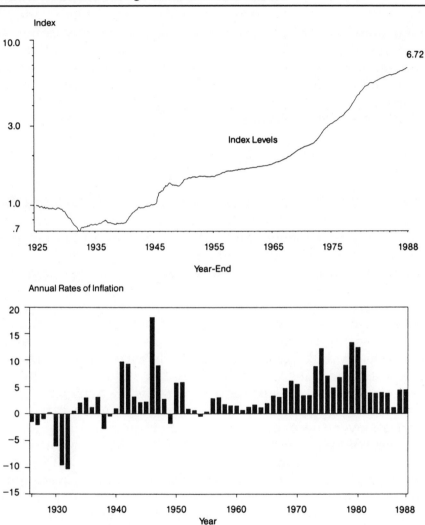

Source: Roger G. Ibbotson and Rex A. Sinquefield, *Stocks, Bonds, Bills, and Inflation* (SBBI), 1982, updated in *SBBI 1989 Yearbook,* Ibbotson Associates, Chicago.

The persistent inflation following World War II was not confined to the United States alone. It has been a world-wide phenomenon, to varying degrees, in different countries at different times. Governments are a primary beneficiary of inflation. This is in part caused by tax structures that tax nominal rather than real income, thus resulting in a shift of wealth from the private to the public sector. Our country's persistent budget deficits are evidence that our government's revenue often fails to cover expenditures with the difference funded predominantly by issuing debt instruments. For the entire 63-year period, inflation had a compound annual rate of 3.1 percent, ranging from a low of −10.3 percent in 1932 to a high of 18.2 percent in 1946.

TREASURY BILLS

Treasury bills are short-term loans to the U.S. Treasury Department. They are sold at a discount from their maturity value, pay no coupons, and have maturities up to one year. Because they are a direct obligation of the federal government, they are free of default risk. The lender is assured that his money will be returned with interest upon maturity. Even though the rate of return on Treasury bills varies from period to period, at the time of purchase the return is known with certainty. Figure 2–3 shows that $1.00 invested in Treasury bills at the end of 1925 with reinvestment of interest grew to be worth $8.93 by the end of 1988. The average compound rate of return over this 63-year period was 3.5 percent, compared with an average inflation rate of 3.1 percent over the same time period. Figure 2–3 also shows the year-by-year pattern of returns on Treasury bills. Despite the modest nominal returns from Treasury bills during the late 1920s and early 1930s, the real returns were quite high because of the deflationary environment. During the 1940s the federal government pegged Treasury bill yields at low levels during a period of higher inflation, with the result that real interest rates were negative. Treasury bill yields were deregulated in 1951, and since then yields have followed inflation rates more closely. Over the entire 63-year period, returns ranged from a low of 0 percent to a high of 14.7 percent.

The Treasury bill's safety and stability of principal value are its great virtues. The price paid for these advan-

FIGURE 2-3
U.S. Treasury Bills: Returns, Return Indices, and Yields (1926–1988)

Source: Roger G. Ibbotson and Rex A. Sinquefield, *Stocks, Bonds, Bills, and Inflation* (SBBI), 1982, updated in *SBBI 1989 Yearbook,* Ibbotson Associates, Chicago.

tages is a rate of return only marginally ahead of inflation. It should be noted that these are pre-tax performance numbers. Had the Treasury bill returns been adjusted downward for payment of income taxes, the performance would have lagged considerably behind inflation. The investment implication is clear. For a Treasury bill investor to stay whole in real terms, he would have to live in a tax-free world and never draw on the interest earned for meeting his living expenses.

When the combined effects of inflation and taxation are considered, Treasury bills and other forms of short-term interest-bearing securities are not riskless investments. Consider the situation of a 50-year-old widow, as summarized in Table 2–1. If she is of average health, she has a life expectancy of approximately 30 more years. Let us assume that certificate of deposit (CD) interest rates are at 8 percent, with an underlying average inflation rate of approximately 7 percent. With $400,000 available for investment, CDs could provide her with $32,000 of annual income. Assume that she never touches a penny's worth of principal but fully uses the interest income for her living expenses. Over the next decade the cost of living will double, reducing the purchasing power of her $400,000 in half to $200,000. Her $32,000 income stream likewise loses half of its value, and can purchase only $16,000 worth of goods and services. Continuing in this same manner over the remaining two decades of her life expectancy, the purchasing power of her initial $400,000 drops to only $50,000, with an annual income stream capable of purchasing only $4,000 worth of goods and services.

Many investors who fear the risks associated with equity investments seek what they perceive to be a safe haven in short-term interest-generating investments. This illustra-

TABLE 2–1
Thirty-Year Life Expectancy (Widow Age 50, Average Health, 8.0% Certificate of Deposit Interest Rates, 7.2% Average Inflation, $400,000 Available for Investment)

Year	Capital Purchasing Power	CD Rate	Real Yield
Now	$400,000	.08	$32,000
10	200,000	.08	16,000
20	100,000	.08	8,000
30	50,000	.08	4,000

tion can be effectively used to underscore the purchasing-power risk inherent in such investments. Often investors are not sufficiently sensitive to the issue of inflation because of the insidious way that inflation takes its toll. Although investors should be concerned primarily with their real returns (i.e., returns adjusted for inflation), often they seem more interested in their nominal results. For example, during the high interest rate environment, 1979 through 1981, Treasury bill returns averaged 12.1 percent, which produced an 8.5 percent after-tax return for a 30 percent marginal-tax-bracket investor. Inflation over the same time period averaged 11.5 percent, producing a Treasury bill after-tax real *loss* of 3 percent per year. Three years later many of these same investors were complaining as they saw average Treasury bill returns from 1982 through 1984 decline to 9.7 percent, which equated to a 6.8 percent after-tax return for the same 30 percent marginal-tax-bracket investor. These returns were achieved, however, during a period when inflation averaged 3.9 percent, thus providing them with a positive real return after taxes of nearly 3 percent per year. Investors need to clearly understand the money illusion of wealth accumulating, when in fact it may be eroding.

Of course, there are other ways to lend money at interest for short periods of time. Commercial paper is unsecured short-term promissory notes issued by corporations. Historically, commercial paper has produced yields of .5 percent to 1 percent more than U.S. Treasury bills. In general, cash equivalents, defined as any short-term interest-bearing security, share many of the same advantages and disadvantages possessed by Treasury bills. Although the real return from cash equivalents will fluctuate from positive to negative, on average it is expected that they will produce pre-tax returns of approximately 1 percent above the inflation rate.

BONDS

Bonds are negotiable promissory notes of a corporation or government entity. They usually pay a series of interest payments followed by a return of principal at maturity. The par value (face value) of a bond appears on the front of the bond certificate and is ordinarily the amount the issuing company initially borrowed and promises to repay at maturity. The coupon rate is the stated rate of interest on a bond which when multiplied by the par value determines the annual interest payments to be paid. The market price of a bond is usually different from its face value. A variety of factors determines the market price of a bond, including the current interest rate environment, the bond's coupon rate, creditworthiness, maturity date, call provisions, and tax status. Bonds are often referred to as *fixed income securities*. The term is somewhat misleading. Only the maximum payment is fixed, not the income paid. In the case of some corporate bonds, for example, interest payments are not always paid as promised.

Bond prices depend in large measure on the prevailing interest rate environment. The fluctuation in bond prices, due to changes in interest rates, is referred to as *interest rate risk*. When first exposed to the concept, many clients may be puzzled by the inverse relationship between interest rates and bond prices. A simple illustration can clarify the concept. Suppose an investor purchases a newly issued 20-year corporate bond at its $10,000 par value. The bond has a 10 percent coupon rate, providing the investor with $1,000 of interest payments annually. Over the following year the interest rate environment increases such that similar newly issued 20-year corporate bonds must provide an 11 percent coupon bond payment in order to entice investors to purchase them. If the holder of the 10 percent coupon bond wants to sell it in this higher interest rate environment, he will find that no one is willing to pay him his original $10,000 purchase price. There is no incentive to buy a $1,000 per year stream of interest payments when the same $10,000 will buy a $1,100 per year stream of interest payments, given the higher interest rates prevailing. The 10 percent coupon bond clearly has value, however, and its price in the marketplace will decline until it reaches a level where the $1,000 payment on the lower market value coupled with the return of face value at maturity is as attractive as the $1,100 annual interest payments on the newly issued $10,000 bond.

The discount rate that equates the present value of the bond's stream of future cash flows (interest payments plus return of principal) to the bond's current market value is the bond's *yield to maturity*. (Mathematically it is the bond's internal rate of return.) The yield to maturity is often simply referred to as the *yield* and takes into consideration the annual interest payments, the number of years to maturity, and the difference between the bond's purchase price and its redemption value at maturity. The yield to maturity must be differentiated from the current yield of a bond, which is simply the annual interest payments divided by the current market price of the bond. The yield to maturity on a bond will be greater than the current yield when the market value of the bond is less than its par value. This is because the yield to maturity takes into consideration the average annual increase in the bond's value as it approaches full par value at maturity. Conversely, the yield to maturity on a bond will be less than the current yield when the market value of the bond is greater than its par value.

Bond investors can choose from a wide variety of alternatives. The characteristics of bonds can most easily be described along three dimensions: interest-rate-risk sensitivity, creditworthiness, and tax status. Interest-rate-risk sensitivity refers to the magnitude of price changes induced by movements in interest rates. As a first approximation, the maturity of a bond is a rough indicator of how sensitive its price will be to interest rate changes. All other things being equal, the longer the maturity, the more the bond price will fluctuate for a given interest rate movement. The marketplace normally prices bonds with various maturities such that longer-maturity bonds with more price sensitivity have higher yields than shorter-maturity securities which have more stable principal values. This gives rise to the normal upward-sloping yield curve, as shown in Figure 2-4. The yield curve plots the relationship between bond yields and corresponding maturities.[1]

---

[1]Duration is a better measure of interest-rate-risk sensitivity than maturity. A discussion of duration and an example of how it is calculated are contained in the Appendix to this chapter.

FIGURE 2-4
Normal Yield Curve

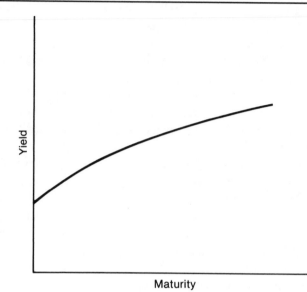

When we discussed the historical performance of Treasury bills, we commented that their returns tend to follow
short-term movements in the inflation rate. Longer-term
yields, however, are not as sensitive to changes in annual
inflation rates because the yield on a long-term bond reflects consensus expectations regarding inflation over the
entire life of the bond. This results in less volatility on the
long-maturity portion of the yield curve. For example, historically a 1 percent change in the yield to maturity for
one-year bonds has been associated with .6 percent and .3
percent changes in yield to maturity, respectively, for three-
and six-year-maturity bonds. Interest-rate-risk sensitivity is
an extremely important concept for a client to understand.
It makes even U.S. government bonds risky and is, therefore, as important to consider as the creditworthiness of a
bond.

The creditworthiness of a bond concerns the likelihood
that payments of interest and return of principal will be

made as promised. Direct government obligations, such as Treasury bills and Treasury bonds, are backed by the full faith and credit of the federal government and are considered to be free of default risk. Corporate bonds, however, have varying degrees of creditworthiness, and their yields to maturity vary accordingly, with the highest yields associated with those bonds that have the highest possibility of default.

The last dimension concerns the tax status of the bond. Certain kinds of municipal bonds issued by local and state governments are free from federal income taxes and can be issued at lower yields. Corporate and federal government bonds, however, generate interest income fully subject to federal income taxes. For high-tax-bracket investors, municipal securities should always be considered in addition to taxable obligations. Let us now review the historical performance of long-term government bonds, intermediate-term government bonds, and long-term corporate bonds.

LONG-TERM GOVERNMENT BONDS

Long-term government bonds are direct obligations of the U.S. government and are regarded as the highest creditworthy issues obtainable. The following performance numbers are based on the construction of a portfolio containing one bond with a reasonably current coupon and a remaining term to maturity of approximately 20 years. Figure 2–1 traces the cumulative performance of a one dollar investment in long-term government bonds in comparison with other investment alternatives. Figure 2–5 shows the long-term government bonds' return indices for total returns versus capital appreciation only. The total return index shows the combined effect of bond price movements coupled with reinvestment of income. In measuring the total annual return from a government bond, the income earned from the bond is added to the change in the price of the bond before the resulting sum is divided by the value of the bond at the beginning of the time period. The capital ap-

FIGURE 2–5
Long-Term Government Bonds: Returns, Return Indices, and Yields
(1926–1988)

Source: Roger G. Ibbotson and Rex A. Sinquefield, *Stocks, Bonds, Bills, and Inflation* (SBBI), 1982, updated in *SBBI 1989 Yearbook*, Ibbotson Associates, Chicago.

preciation return is defined to be the total return minus the bond's yield to maturity. The capital appreciation index accordingly reflects only bond price changes caused by interest rate movements. The only way an investor can be assured of receiving the current yield to maturity on a long-term government bond is by holding the bond until maturity. If it is sold prior to maturity, an intervening interest rate movement will produce a corresponding capital gain or capital loss, making the investor's actual return vary.

As we lengthen the time horizon over which we lend money to the government through the purchase of a long-term government bond, we leave behind the stable principal value characteristic of short-term Treasury bills. Interest rate risk now enters the equation. Given that risk, we expect to be compensated for bearing it, in the form of a higher yield on our invested dollar. In Figure 2–5, we see that $1.00 invested in long-term government bonds at the end of 1925 grew to be worth $14.64, with full reinvestment of income, by the end of 1988. This is a compound annual return of 4.4 percent. This surpasses the Treasury bills' corresponding 1988 ending value of $8.93, produced by a compound return of 3.5 percent. As a result of the interest rate risk of long-term government bonds, the returns were much more volatile than those of Treasury bills, ranging from a low of −9.2 percent in 1967, to a high of 40.3 percent in 1982.

In working with clients, there is a danger in focusing too much attention on the relationships among long-term average returns without discussing the variations in performance which occur over shorter time periods. To facilitate this historical review, let us consider three decidedly different periods. The first is 1926 through the conclusion of World War II in 1945. The second is 1946 through the interest rate cycle peak of 1981. The third is the disinflationary period 1982 through the end of 1988.

From 1926 through 1945, the average compound inflation rate was less than .1 percent because of the deflation that existed for the first several years of this period. This can be seen clearly in Figure 2–2 which traces the CPI from its initial $1.00 value in 1926 down to a low of $.73 in 1932 before rising again to just over $1.00 by the end of 1945. The superior performance of bonds is evident by the steady rise in value shown in Figure 2-5. Government bonds performed exceedingly well and provided investors with a compound annual growth rate of 4.7 percent. Because the average inflation rate was close to zero, bonds had a real compound return almost identical to their nominal compound return. By comparison, Treasury bills had a compound return of 1.1 percent. By the end of 1945, $1.00 invested in government bonds with full reinvestment of income had grown to be worth $2.51—more than twice as much as a $1.00 investment in Treasury bills which grew to be worth $1.24. An examination of the bottom graph in Figure 2-5 shows that yields were relatively stable during this period and trended down within a relatively narrow range of 2.0 percent to 4.0 percent. The downward trend produced a corresponding appreciation in bond prices. This can be clearly identified on the top graph in Figure 2-5 which shows the capital appreciation index reaching a maximum for the entire 63-year period of $1.42 by the end of this period. The middle chart in Figure 2-5 shows the pattern of total annual returns. This confirms the positive performance achieved during this time period. With the notable exception of 1931, when government bonds had a total return of −5.3 percent, total annual returns during this two-decade time period were positive.

During the second period, which extends from the beginning of 1946 through the end of 1981, government bonds experienced a prolonged bear market. Figure 2-2 shows a brief period following World War II during which inflation increased sharply, then leveled off for two decades before beginning its prolonged acceleration from the 1970's through the end of 1981. Over the entire period, the compound annual inflation rate was 4.7 percent. Short-term interest rates and Treasury bill returns lagged inflation during the first portion of this period, as a result of the federal government's action in pegging interest rates at artificially low levels. Following deregulation of Treasury bill rates, however, Treasury bill returns closely mirrored the accelerating inflation/interest rate environment, which characterized this period. The bottom graph in Figure 2–5 shows a pattern of increasing yields pushed by an accelerating inflationary environment. The middle graph shows frequent occurrences of negative total annual returns during years when the interest payments on the bond were not large enough to offset the bond's price loss for the year. The compound annual return with reinvestment of income for the entire period was 2.0 percent—less than half that of Treasury bills' compound annual return of 4.1 percent. Current yields obviously were much higher, indicating that the low total return was caused by a protracted capital loss. Without the reinvestment of income, the investment experience of long-term government bondholders was devastating. The capital appreciation component of long-term government bonds' cumulative return, which had reached its peak of $1.42 at the end of 1945, declined to its 63-year low of $.48 by the end of 1981. This was a principal loss of nearly two thirds, before one considers the additional damage imposed by inflation. (Refer to the top graph in Figure 2–5.) The interest rate risk that worked for government bondholders prior to 1946 was working against them from 1946 through the end of 1981. A government bond's yield has three components: an inflation component, a real riskless interest rate, and a premium for bearing interest rate risk. A policy of consistently spending all three components is a prescription for long-term trouble. No period of history more clearly demonstrates the danger of buying "safe" long-term government bonds and using the interest for living expenses.

As Treasury bill returns were peaking in 1981 at a historical high of 14.7 percent, many investors were swearing that they would never again invest in long-term government bonds. The premium they expected to receive for bearing interest rate risk had not been delivered. The deterioration in bond performance had been so dramatic that by the end of 1981, the post-1925 cumulative performance of Treasury bills actually surpassed that of long-term government bonds. This can be seen in Figure 2–1 where the inflation, Treasury bill, and long-term government bond lines converge.

The final period begins in 1982. Inflation and interest rates both dropped precipitously, producing huge gains in long-term government bond prices. The magnitude of these gains is appreciated if one examines the middle graph in Figure 2–5, which shows the pattern of total annual returns. During the 56-year period leading up to 1982, there were only two years, 1932 and 1976, when the total return on long-term government bonds exceeded 15 percent. Then, in 1982 long-term government bonds had a total return of 40 percent, followed later by total returns of 15 percent, 31 percent, and 24 percent successively in 1984, 1985, and 1986! Given the disinflationary environment, Treasury bill returns were declining as expected, but were nevertheless very high in real terms by historical standards. A comparison of the performance of long-term government bonds for the first versus the second half of the decade ending with 1986 provides an interesting contrast of the good and bad aspects of interest rate risk, coupled with the impact of inflation. Every long-term bond investor should sign a statement indicating that he has seen and understands the information presented in Table 2–2. In a changing interest rate environment, long-term debt obligations are definitely risky.

During the entire 63-year period, long-term government bonds provided a compound annual return of 4.4 percent. This is considerably ahead of Treasury bills and inflation,

TABLE 2–2
Comparative Bond Performance

Five-year Period	(A) Long-term Govt. Bond Compound Return	(B) Compound Rate of Inflation	(C) = (A) − (B) Inflation Adjusted Compound Return of Long-term Govt. Bonds
1977 through 1981	−1.0%	10.1%	−11.1%
1982 through 1986	21.6	3.3	18.3

Source: Based on data from Roger G. Ibbotson and Rex A. Sinquefield, *Stocks, Bonds, Bills, and Inflation* (SBBI), 1982, updated in *SBBI 1989 Yearbook*, Ibbotson Associates, Chicago.

but it took the experience of several spectacular bond years since 1981 for these relative performance relationships to re-develop. We have seen that during periods of deflation and disinflation, long-term government bonds provide excellent returns. During periods of moderate inflation, returns are good provided that the inflation is anticipated. During peri-ods of high inflation, however, long-term government bonds, as well as other long-term debt obligations, do poorly.

INTERMEDIATE-TERM GOVERNMENT BONDS

The return indices, total annual returns, and yields for intermediate-term government bonds are found in Figure 2-6. The data used for constructing this exhibit describes the performance of a noncallable bond, with the shortest maturity of not less than five years. These bonds have less interest-rate-risk sensitivity than long-term government bonds because of their shorter maturities. The expectation, therefore, is that intermediate-term bonds should produce to-tal returns less than that of long-term government bonds, but more than that of Treasury bills. Surprisingly, Figure 2-6 shows that $1.00 invested in intermediate-term govern-ment bonds, with full reinvestment of income, grew to be worth $18.98 by the end of 1988. This represents a com-pound annual return of 4.8 percent, which is greater than the compound annual return of 4.4 percent produced by long-term government bonds. In comparing the portion of the total return attributed to the income reinvested, we find that as expected, long-term government bonds' income re-turn of 4.8 percent was greater than the 4.5 percent pro-duced by intermediate-term government bonds. The under-performance of long-term government bonds can therefore be traced to the greater interest-rate-risk sensitivity associ-ated with their longer maturity. The interest rate environ-ment in the latter part of the 63-year period was higher than at the beginning. This produced a substantial cap-ital loss for long-term government bonds. The higher in-

FIGURE 2-6
Intermediate-Term Government Bonds: Returns, Return Indices, and Yields
(1926–1988)

Source: Roger G. Ibbotson and Rex A. Sinquefield, *Stocks, Bonds, Bills, and Inflation* (SBBI), 1982, updated in *SBBI 1989 Yearbook,* Ibbotson Associates, Chicago.

come return from long-term government bonds was not sufficient to overcome the magnitude of this capital loss, and therefore intermediate-term government bonds outperformed long-term government bonds.

Had the actual inflation and interest rate rise been fully anticipated by the marketplace, yields would have been higher on long-term government bonds with the result that principal values would not have deteriorated. Had this been the case, the 4.4 percent compound annual return produced historically by long-term government bonds would have to be increased by the average capital loss to produce an adjusted compound annual return which would have surpassed that provided by intermediate-term government bonds. It is very interesting to note that during this period of generally rising interest rates, intermediate-term government bonds nevertheless appreciated at an average compound rate of .1 percent. Some possible explanations for this are discussed in the Appendix to this chapter.

Although the upside on intermediate-term government bonds is less spectacular than that of long-term government bonds, the downside is correspondingly less. For example, over the 63-year period 1926 through 1988, intermediate-term government bonds had negative total returns in only 6 years, compared to 18 years of negative total returns for long-term government bonds.

LONG-TERM CORPORATE BONDS

As with long-term government bonds, long-term corporate bonds have long maturities. They are therefore subject to interest rate risk, and investors deserve a corresponding horizon premium for bearing it. Unlike long-term government bonds, however, long-term corporate bonds have credit risk. Investors lack complete certainty that all payments of interest and principal will be made as promised. If held to maturity, a government bond will provide an investor with an expected return equal to the bond's yield to maturity. But because corporate bonds have a possibility of default, the expected return will be less than the yield to maturity. To compensate investors for bearing this credit risk, the return on corporate bonds, after adjustment for any defaults, should be in excess of that available from long-term government bonds. We will call this compensation the *default premium* and define it as the difference between the return on government bonds and the return on corporate bonds with similar maturity after any necessary adjustment for losses due to defaults.

Figure 2-7 shows the pattern of total annual returns, as well as the return indices, for long-term corporate bonds. The bonds used in compiling this data series are Aaa- and Aa-rated bonds with maturities of approximately 20 years. As with government bonds, total returns are equal to capital appreciation plus reinvested income. Based on the 63 years of data compiled by Ibbotson Associates, the default premium historically has been .6 percent compounded annually. This is derived by subtracting long-term government bonds' compound annual return of 4.4 percent from the 5.0 percent compound annual return produced by long-term corporate bonds. This higher return with corporate bonds produced a 1988 ending value of $21.90 for an initial investment of $1.00 with reinvestment of income.

Corporate bonds vary widely in terms of their creditworthiness, with lower-quality bonds having higher expected returns than high-quality bonds. Returns on low-quality bonds are more volatile because of their greater sensitivity to movements in stock prices. Historically, medium- to lower-grade bonds have provided investors with higher net returns over time after adjustment for all capital losses.

COMMON STOCKS

Common stock represents ownership interest in a corporation. Investors who buy a share of common stock buy a piece of the company. Unlike fixed income securities, common stocks

FIGURE 2-7
Long-Term Corporate Bonds: Returns and Return Indices (1926–1988)

Source: Roger G. Ibbotson and Rex A. Sinquefield, *Stocks, Bonds, Bills, and Inflation* (SBBI), 1982, updated in *SBBI 1989 Yearbook,* Ibbotson Associates, Chicago.

have neither fixed maturity dates nor fixed schedules of promised payments. Out of its revenues, a corporation must first pay its expenses, including what it owes to bondholders and other creditors. Obviously, a corporation's creditors have greater certainty regarding their payment than do its shareholders. Common stocks are therefore more risky than fixed income securities. Because the bondholders and other creditors of a corporation have a prior claim to the corporation's revenues and assets, common stock shareholders are said to have a *residual ownership interest*. The return to a shareholder is in the form of dividends and/or capital appreciation. Dividends are paid in accordance with the decisions of the board of directors, which is elected by the shareholders. The portion of earnings not paid out in dividends is available for reinvestment by the corporation and provides one source of financing for the future growth of the enterprise. Like any business owner, common stock shareholders share in both the upside potential and downside risk of the corporation. For assuming greater risk, common stock shareholders expect greater rewards over time. Stock market prices in general reflect investors' assessment of the state of the economy. The better the economic outlook for business, the higher the level of stock prices.

The common stock performance numbers used for Figures 2-1 and 2-8 are based upon the Standard & Poor's 500 Stock Composite Index (S&P 500). The S&P 500 presently includes 500 of the largest U.S. stocks, as measured in terms of the total market value of shares outstanding. One dollar invested in common stocks, with reinvestment of income, grew rapidly from the end of 1925 until it reached a value of $2.20 by the end of 1928. The stock market crash and Great Depression followed, taking stock prices down for the next four years. By the end of 1932, the total return index reached its 63-year low of $.79. By comparison, government and corporate bonds were performing quite well. By the end of 1944 common stocks had made up their lost ground with the total return index reaching $2.91, thereby surpassing the $2.82 total return index for the best performing interest-generating alternative—long-term corporate bonds. From that point

FIGURE 2-8
Common Stocks: Returns, Return Indices, and Yields (1926–1988)

Source: Roger G. Ibbotson and Rex A. Sinquefield, *Stocks, Bonds, Bills, and Inflation* (SBBI), 1982, updated in *SBBI 1989 Yearbook,* Ibbotson Associates, Chicago.

forward through the end of 1988, the total return index for common stocks would maintain its cumulative performance advantage over corporate bonds, government bonds, and Treasury bills. Although there would be common stock bear markets, most notably in 1973–1974, which would at times narrow the lead, the long-term secular trend was one of an increasing performance advantage for common stocks.

The last several years of this period are particularly noteworthy. The bull market, which began in the middle of 1982, produced an advance of more than 260 percent before peaking five years later. Although this was not the largest bull market advance on record, it was the most rapid prolonged gain. Measured from the trough to the peak, the total return on common stocks was nearly 30 percent compounded annually. This historical first was followed by another. On October 19, 1987, the stock market crashed, with prices falling more than 20 percent—the largest single-day decline on record. At the end of 1988, the common stock total return index had a value of $406.45, produced by a 63-year compound total return of 10.0 percent annually. This performance completely dominated the compound annual returns over the same period of 5.0 percent, 4.4 percent, 4.8 percent, and 3.5 percent for long-term corporate bonds, long-term government bonds, intermediate-term government bonds, and U.S. Treasury bills, respectively.

The "miracle of compound interest" is quite apparent when one realizes that common stocks had a compound return of only 6 percent to 7 percent in excess of Treasury bills, yet produced nearly 46 times the accumulated wealth during the 63-year period. The dramatic superior long-term performance of common stocks is matched by a correspondingly higher volatility in annual returns. This is evident by a visual comparison of the total return indices for common stocks versus long-term government bonds and Treasury bills in Figure 2–1. The center graph in Figure 2–8 also highlights this volatility by showing the year-by-year pattern of total annual returns.

When we examined the historical performance of corporate bonds, government bonds, and Treasury bills, we saw that these investment alternatives could outpace inflation only by reinvesting their income returns. This was not true, however, with common stocks. Figure 2–8 shows that the capital appreciation return index had a 1988 ending value of $21.77, which is considerably more than the $6.72 CPI value. Thus, even if the dividend yield was spent for consumption, common stocks' capital appreciation would have on average stayed ahead of inflation. In this sense, it is reasonable to consider common stocks to be a long-term "inflation indexed investment." This is not surprising, given the long-term real growth of the economy. Assume, for example, that during the next decade we have annual inflation of 7.2 percent, which will double the price of goods and services within the economy. If we presume that the corporations that produce these goods and services maintain the same level of production over the next decade, and have the same profit margins and price-earnings ratios for their common stocks then as now, then corporate earnings and share prices will likewise double, even if all earnings are paid out as dividends. As with bonds, anticipated inflation is priced into the expected return of common stocks. But with common stocks our performance expectations are different. We expect a broadly diversified common stock portfolio to maintain its purchasing power (i.e., keep up with inflation) while simultaneously generating a stream of dividends which may start out at a modest level, but can likewise grow to maintain its purchasing power on average over time. By contrast, bonds promise only the return of principal in nominal terms, with a fixed income return that is initially higher than the average dividend yield available from common stocks but which is fixed as to its upper limit. In essence, with bonds' other promises, you also have the assurance that your principal will lose to inflation.

Historically, stocks do much better in a low-inflationary environment where there is relative stability in consumer prices. Performance has been poor during periods of either deflation or high inflation. It is the *unanticipated* inflation that is especially harmful to common stock performance—particularly in the short-run. Over longer periods of time, corporations can make adjustments to inflation, but in the short-run these adjustments are more difficult to accomplish. It is logical to project that barring the collapse of the economic system as we know it, common stocks as an investment vehicle will provide a good alternative for the long-term preservation and enhancement of purchasing power.

SMALL COMPANY STOCKS

The long-term superior performance of small stocks, relative to all other investment alternatives we have discussed thus far, is evident in Figure 2-1. The stocks used to compile this wealth index are those comprising the fifth (smallest) quintile of the New York Stock Exchange, where stocks are ranked by their market capitalization (market price × number of shares outstanding). One dollar invested in small stocks at the end of 1925 grew to be worth $1,478.14 with full reinvestment of income by the end of 1988. This represents a compound annual return of 12.3 percent, compared with the next best result of 10.0 percent achieved by larger capitalization common stocks. We will call the 2.3 percent difference between small and large company stock performance the *small stock premium.* There are several possible explanations for the superior performance of small stocks. A comparison of the pattern of total annual returns, as shown on the bottom graph of Figure 2-9, reveals more volatility than that demonstrated by large company stock returns. An increased return for small company stocks is consistent with their higher volatility. Also, small stocks tend to have higher betas, making them more susceptible to overall stock market movements, and thereby again justifying higher returns. Finally, one could argue that large capitalization companies may tend to be in more mature businesses, with their periods of rapid growth behind and not ahead of them. Yet, there is evidence that small stocks do even better than one would expect, given their betas and overall volatility.

FIGURE 2-9
Small Company Stocks: Returns and Return Indices (1926–1988)

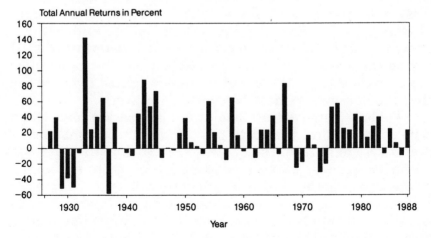

Source: Roger G. Ibbotson and Rex A. Sinquefield, *Stocks, Bonds, Bills, and Inflation* (SBBI), 1982, updated in *SBBI 1989 Yearbook,* Ibbotson Associates, Chicago.

Academicians used the term *market anomaly* to describe a situation such as this where the returns are different from what is expected. One explanation of this anomaly is that there may be factors other than market risk, important in the pricing of small company stocks. Those who conclude that the risk-adjusted returns are indeed better for small company stocks, however, can exploit the anomaly and capture the excess return by substituting small company stocks for large company stocks having similar characteristics such as beta, yield, and industry sector.

APPENDIX: BOND DURATION

Maturity is not the preferred measure of interest-rate-risk sensitivity because it considers only the timing of repayment of principal upon maturity. Maturity accordingly ignores the timing and magnitude of interest payments made in the interim. Because a major portion of the present value of a bond may be attributed to the interest payments, a better measure would take these payments into consideration as well. A bond's "duration" is a measurement that accomplishes this. It is calculated as the weighted average of the lengths of time prior to receipt of interest payments and return of principal, where each payment's weight is determined by dividing its present value by the current market value of the bond. In short, it is the present value weighted average time that the bondholder has money owed to him.

Table 2-3 shows the calculation of duration for a 10 percent coupon bond priced to provide an 11 percent yield to maturity. The duration of 2.73 years is less than the three-year maturity, because of the consideration given to the interim interest payments. Had this calculation been performed for a three-year-maturity zero coupon bond, 100 percent of the weighting would have been given to the single-payment return of principal at maturity, and accordingly, the duration would have been equal to the maturity of three years.

TABLE 2-3
Calculation of Bond Duration

Par value			$10,000	
Coupon rate			10%	
Interest payments			$1,000 annually	
Years to maturity			3	
Current market value of bond			$9,756	
Yield to maturity			11%	

(1)	(2)	(3)	(4)	(5)
Years from Now	Payment	Present Value of Payment at 11%	Present Value of Payment as a Percentage of the Current Market Value of the Bond	Column (1) Times Column (4)
1	$ 1,000 I	$ 901	.092	.092
2	1,000 I	812	.083	.166
3	1,000 I	731	.075	.225
	10,000 P	7,312	.749	2.247
		$9,756		2.73*

I = Interest
P = Principal
* = Duration in years

Because duration is a better indicator of interest-rate-risk sensitivity, a group of bonds with the same duration, but varying maturities, will respond similarly to a given interest rate move, whereas a different group of bonds with the same maturity, but with different durations, will have varying price sensitivities. Duration most accurately reflects interest-rate-risk sensitivity for bonds whose prices are close to par. For example, for a bond with an eight-year duration, 10.0 percent yield, and a market value equal to par, a 50 basis point decrease in the yield to a 9.5 percent would cause the price of the bond to increase by approximately eight times 50 basis points, or 4.0 percent to $10,400.

Earlier in the chapter, we commented that despite the rising interest rate environment, intermediate-term government bonds appreciated at a compound annual rate of .1 percent from 1926 through 1988. This may partly result from some unusual characteristics of the bonds selected in building the intermediate-term government bond data series. Another possible explanation involves the positive convexity of most bonds. Positive convexity produces a higher return on average than would be expected, given a bond's yield. This is caused by an inverse relationship between a bond's duration and the direction of interest rate movements. An increase in bond yields has the effect of shortening a bond's duration. (This occurs because of a corresponding increase in the discount rate used in computing the present value weights for the bond payments.) This in turn makes the bond less susceptible to further capital loss. Conversely, a decrease in bond yields lengthens duration and thereby makes the bond more susceptible to price change. The changes in duration caused by movements in interest rates are advantageous to the bondholder in both rising and falling interest rate markets. This produces realized returns that are better than would be expected, given the bond's yield.

CHAPTER 3

COMPARATIVE RELATIONSHIPS AMONG CAPITAL MARKET INVESTMENT ALTERNATIVES

> The best way to suppose what may come is to remember what is passed.
> —*George Savile, Marquess of Halifax* (1633–1695)
> Political, Moral and Miscellaneous Reflections, 1750

MODELS FOR THE EXPECTED RETURNS FROM CAPITAL MARKET INVESTMENT ALTERNATIVES

Treasury bills historically have had a compound annual return of 3.5 percent, which is .4 percent more than the corresponding compound annual inflation rate of 3.1 percent. Some researchers have concluded on this basis that the real (i.e., inflation-adjusted) riskless interest rate is therefore .4 percent. Accepting that assumption, we can use current Treasury bill yields for an approximate indicator of short-term inflation expectations:

Treasury bill yield	=	$z\%$
Minus real riskless interest rate	=	$-.4\%$
Equals the expected short-term inflation rate	=	$(z - .4)\%$

By reorganizing the terms, we can build a simple model of the components of Treasury bill returns:

Expected short-term expected inflation rate	=	$y\%$
Plus the real riskless rate of interest	=	$+ .4\%$
Equals the Treasury bill yield		$= (y + .4)\%$

The interest rate risk associated with long-term government bonds deserves compensation in the form of an extra return over what would be available with Treasury bills. The incremental return for bearing interest rate risk is commonly referred to as the *horizon premium*. Historically, long-term government bonds have had a compound annual return of 4.4 percent, compared with the 3.5 percent compound annual return produced by Treasury bills. This indicates an incremental compound annual horizon premium of .9 percent. We know that the pricing mechanism of the marketplace builds into the bond's yield compensation for the risks associated with *anticipated* inflation and interest rate movements. In essence, although investors expect that their bond portfolios will fluctuate in principal value, they do not expect long-term permanent principal losses. Long-term government bonds, however, experienced a prolonged period of substantial unanticipated inflation with a corresponding secular rise in interest rates. This eroded principal values at a compound annual rate of $-.7$ percent. For this reason, the historical compound horizon premium of .9 percent is lower than what would have been expected had bonds preserved their nominal values. An expected horizon premium can be inferred from the historical data by adjusting for bonds' long-term loss in principal value. This adjustment would indicate an expected horizon premium of 1.6 percent computed as follows:

Compound annual return from long-term government bonds	=	4.4%
Minus compound annual return from Treasury bills	=	$- 3.5\%$
Equals the historical compound annual return horizon premium	=	.9%
Plus an adjustment for the compound annual loss of principal value	=	$+ .7\%$
Equals the expected horizon premium	=	1.6%

An argument can be made that the greater volatility of long-term government bond returns since 1979 may justify, and may have resulted in, a larger horizon premium as a consequence of an increase in interest rate risk. For our purposes, however, we will assume that the 1.6 percent expected horizon premium is a good estimate for the future. On this basis, it is reasonable to expect that on average, Treasury bills will provide a compound return of .4 percent in excess of the inflation rate, while long-term government bonds will have a compound return of 1.6 percent in excess of the current Treasury bill yield. We can now specify a model for the expected total return on long-term government bonds:

Treasury bill yield	=	$x\%$
Plus the expected horizon premium	=	$+ 1.6\%$
Equals the expected total return on long-term government bonds	=	$(x + 1.6)\%$

If we presume that the default premium will be the same in the future as it has been historically, our model for the components of expected return for long-term corporate bonds is:

Treasury bill yield	=	$x\%$
Plus the expected horizon premium	=	$+ 1.6\%$
Equals the expected total return on long-term government bonds	=	$(x + 1.6)\%$
Plus the expected default premium	=	$+ .6\%$
Equals the expected total return on long-term corporate bonds	=	$(x + 2.2)\%$

During the 63-year period we reviewed, common stocks had a compound annual return of 10.0 percent—6.5 percent more than the compound annual return of 3.5 percent from Treasury bills. The difference between the return from common stocks and the return from Treasury bills is called the *equity risk premium*. If we assume that the risk inherent in common stocks will not be materially different in the future than it has been in the past, and if we further assume that the market will price common stocks such that the compensation for bearing that risk is the same in the future as it has been historically, then 6.5 percent will be a reasonable estimate of the expected equity risk premium in the future. We can thus build a simple model for the expected return for common stocks:

Treasury bill yield	$=$	$x\%$
Plus the expected equity risk premium	$=$	$+\ 6.5\%$
Equals the expected total return on common stocks		$=(x+6.5)\%$

Figure 3–1 shows how the equity risk premium has varied during the past 63 years. Each point on the graph indicates the difference between the compound annual return for the S&P 500 and the compound annual return for Treasury bills for the preceding five-year period. The volatility is quite apparent and serves as a reminder that these models provide only single-point estimates of future security returns. A better description of future performance would incorporate a description of a probabilistic range of outcomes. It is important to share this range of outcomes with the client in order to provide him with a context for evaluating subsequent investment performance.

Finally, with the assumption that the historical small stock premium is a good estimate of the future small stock premium, our model for the expected return on small stocks is:

Treasury bill yield	$=$	$x\%$
Plus the expected equity risk premium	$=$	$+\ 6.5\%$
Equals the expected total return on common stocks	$=$	$(x+6.5)\%$
Plus the expected small stock premium	$=$	$+\ 2.3\%$
Equals the expected total return on small company stocks	$=$	$(x+8.8)\%$

The relationships described in these models are an important part of the foundation for developing the client's understanding of investment risk and return. They also pro-

FIGURE 3-1
Equity Risk Premium (1926–1988)

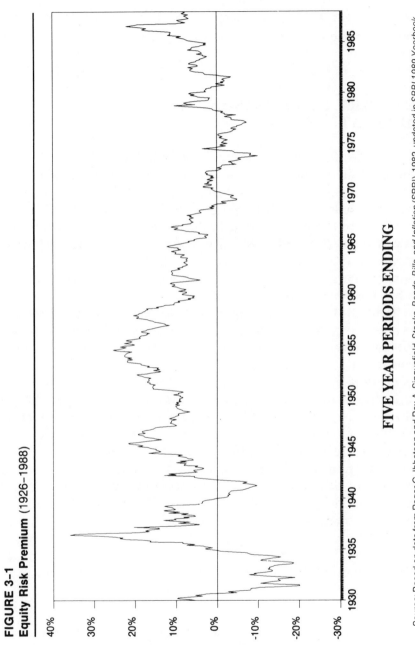

FIVE YEAR PERIODS ENDING

Source: Based on data from Roger G. Ibbotson and Rex A. Sinquefield, *Stocks, Bonds, Bills, and Inflation* (SBBI), 1982, updated in *SBBI 1989 Yearbook*, Ibbotson Associates, Chicago.

vide valuable benchmarks that can help clients to develop
more realistic expectations regarding future investment performance.

SUMMARY COMPARISONS AND IMPLICATIONS

Clients often misperceive the risks they face in the investment of their money. If these misperceptions go uncorrected,
it is very likely that clients will make portfolio decisions that
are not in their best interests. This highlights the value of
providing to the client a detailed historical review of the capital markets. A client who fully understands inflation, interest rate risk, credit risk, and equity risk is in a much better
position to make intelligent investment decisions appropriate
for his long-term objectives.

Table 3-1 provides an excellent summary of the comparative performance of the major investment alternatives we
have reviewed.[1] The column labeled *Geometric Mean* compares the historical compound annual returns for the various
investment alternatives. It is clear that over the long term,
equity investments such as common stocks have had better
returns than bonds, which in turn have outperformed Treasury bills. Correspondingly, we can see, by comparing their
respective standard deviations, that the higher returns have
been obtained at the price of more volatility. In comparing
the returns of these investment alternatives, clients are often surprised by the impact that small incremental returns
have had on wealth accumulation. For example, Treasury
bills, with a compound annual return of 3.5 percent, resulted
in the growth of a $1.00 investment to $8.93 by the end of
1988. By contrast, common stocks had a compound annual

---

[1] If you are unfamiliar with some of the statistical concepts used in this section,
it may be helpful to review the Appendix to this chapter. It provides summary
explanations of the terms: geometric mean, arithmetic mean, expected return,
standard deviation, probability distribution, and first-order autocorrelation.

TABLE 3-1
Summary Statistics of Annual Returns, 1926-1988 (Total Returns, Income, and Capital Appreciation of the Basic Asset Classes)

Series	Geometric Mean	Arithmetic Mean	Standard Deviation	First-order Auto- correlation
Common stocks				
Total returns	10.0%	12.1%	20.9%	.01
Income	4.8	4.8	1.3	.80
Capital appreciation	5.0	7.0	20.1	.00
Small-company stocks				
Total returns	12.3	17.8	35.6	.10
Long-term corporate bonds				
Total returns	5.0	5.3	8.4	.16
Long-term government bonds				
Total returns	4.4	4.7	8.5	.09
Income	4.8	4.9	2.9	.95
Capital appreciation	−0.7	−0.4	7.3	−.02
Intermediate-term government bonds				
Total returns	4.8	4.9	5.5	.28
Income	4.5	4.5	3.3	.93
Capital appreciation	0.1	0.2	4.1	−.05
U.S. Treasury bills				
Total returns	3.5	3.6	3.3	.92
Inflation rates	3.1	3.2	4.8	.64

Source: Roger G. Ibbotson and Rex A. Sinquefield, *Stocks, Bonds, Bills, and Inflation* (SBBI), 1982, updated in *SBBI 1989 Yearbook,* Ibbotson Associates, Chicago.

return of only 6.5 percent more, yet the initial $1.00 investment grew to $406.45 over the same time period. Similarly, small company stocks had an incremental compound annual return of only 2.3 percent in excess of common stocks, yet this small additional return produced an astounding value of $1,478.14 by the end of 1988. These are clear illustrations of the "miracle of compound interest."

Contrasted with these relatively modest incremental differences in compound annual returns, there are wide differences in the standard deviations of returns among the various investment alternatives. For example, Table 3-1 shows that Treasury bills not only had the lowest historical compound return; they also had the lowest standard deviation. The historical variability of return for Treasury bills should not, however, be interpreted as a short-run measure of uncertainty in return. There are two reasons for this. First, average Treasury bill returns have generally trended upward during this time period. This upward long-term movement in average Treasury bill returns produces higher deviations around the long-term average than would be true around the average for a shorter period of time. In this sense, the long-term standard deviation of Treasury bills overstates their historical short-run volatility. Second, it is possible to completely eliminate the short-run uncertainty in return by purchasing a one-year-maturity Treasury bill, and thereby lock in the return. For these reasons, it is inappropriate to consider Treasury bills' long-term standard deviation as an indicator of future volatility.

Contrasted with Treasury bills is common stocks' very high standard deviation of 20.9 percent around its arithmetic mean of 12.1 percent. With the simplifying assumption that common stock returns are normally distributed, roughly two thirds of our yearly return observations should fall within plus or minus 20.9 percent of the arithmetic mean of 12.1 percent. The middle graph in Figure 2–8 shows common stocks' pattern of total annual returns. Imagine, for example, drawing a horizontal line across the graph corresponding to the 12.1 percent arithmetic mean. Then draw another horizontal line one standard deviation above that at 33.0 percent, and another line one standard deviation beneath it at −8.8 percent. These upper and lower horizontal lines form an envelope that contains approximately two thirds of the annual return observations. The other one third of the annual return observations falls outside the envelope.

It is important to emphasize that the high volatility of common stock returns swamps any short-run recognition of the higher return one expects to receive from making an equity investment. Although the wide range of standard deviation numbers shown in Table 3–1 provides a good comparison of relative volatility, a visual comparison is much more striking. Figures 3–2A and 3–2B show the pattern of total annual returns for the various investment alternatives compared directly with each other on a series of graphs with a common vertical scale. This method of presentation gives the client a much better sense of relative volatility.

Table 3–1 breaks down the standard deviation of common stocks' total returns into income and capital appreciation components. It is very interesting to note that the capital appreciation component has a standard deviation of 20.1 percent compared with 1.3 percent for the income component. Clearly, the variability of return associated with common stocks is attributable almost entirely to price movements, with the dividend income component being relatively stable. One possible explanation lies in the manner in which dividend policy is established for most corporations. A corporation's earnings will fluctuate from year to year. Rather than pay a dividend that fluctuates with earnings, however, corporations seek to set dividends at a rate that can be comfortably paid out of earnings through both good and bad years. Corporations do not want to cut a dividend unless cutting is absolutely necessary, and they generally raise dividends only when they are confident that a relatively permanent improvement in earnings justifies a higher payout.[2] This practice leads to a relatively stable and gradually increasing pattern of dividend payouts.

Table 3–1 shows that the capital appreciation component for common stock returns is 5.0 percent. This is equivalent to the *total* return of the best-performing interest-generating alternative—corporate bonds. In essence, a common stock investor historically has had long-term capital appreciation sufficient to not only maintain, but moreover enhance his purchasing power. This leaves the dividend stream available for consumption. Because a common stock portfolio can keep up with inflation on average over time, so will its dividend stream. Emphasis is on the phrase *on average over*

---

[2]For this reason, announcements of dividend changes—good or bad—are said to have *information content* and are of great interest to the investment community.

FIGURE 3–2A
Total Annual Returns in Percent (1926–1988)

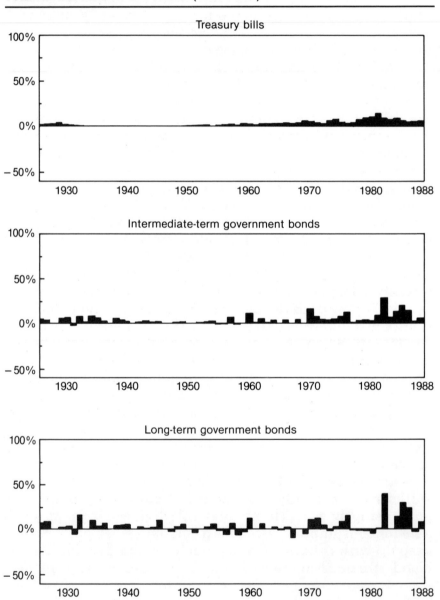

Source: Based on data from Roger G. Ibbotson and Rex A. Sinquefield, *Stocks, Bonds, Bills, and Inflation* (SBBI), 1982, updated in *SBBI 1989 Yearbook*, Ibbotson Associates, Chicago.

FIGURE 3–2B
Total Annual Returns in Percent (1926–1988)

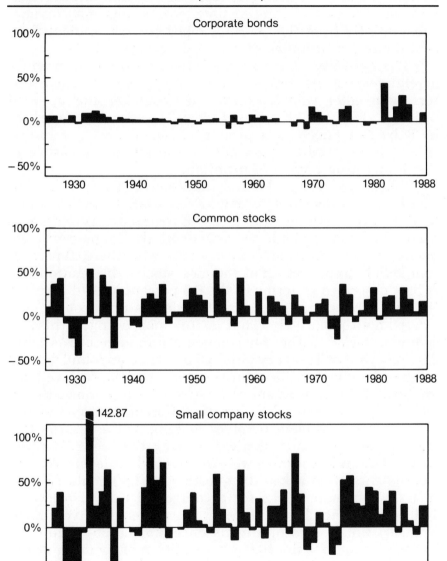

Source: Based on data from Roger G. Ibbotson and Rex A. Sinquefield, *Stocks, Bonds, Bills, and Inflation* (SBBI), 1982, updated in *SBBI 1989 Yearbook,* Ibbotson Associates, Chicago.

time because in the short-run the much higher volatility of common stocks produces great uncertainty in returns. Therefore, short-term and intermediate-term results may diverge substantially from the "normal relationships" indicated by examining performance over longer periods of time.

The capacity of a common stock portfolio to produce a relatively stable, growing dividend stream is important for an investor who is concerned about keeping up with inflation. Had the 50-year-old woman previously described in Table 2-1 allocated a portion of her money to common stocks, her portfolio would not have been so susceptible to the devastating impact of inflation.

When reviewing the information in Table 3-1 with clients, it is important to emphasize that the return numbers should be evaluated in terms of their spreads relative to each other. For example, in comparing the 3.5 percent compound annual return of Treasury bills with the 10.0 percent compound annual return of common stocks, the relationship is best described in terms of the 6.5 percent spread between the two. Occasionally, the relationship is erroneously considered multiplicatively. That is, it is misleading to think of common stocks' 10.0 percent compound annual return as being 2.9 times that of Treasury bills' 3.5 percent compound annual return. (A review of the security-return models we developed for each of the investment alternatives clearly shows the relationships in terms of arithmetic differences or spreads.)

A similar problem involves looking at the returns outside of their historical context. During the late 1970s and early 1980s, interest rates were at double digit levels. At that time, clients often asked the question, "Why should I invest in risky common stocks for a compound rate of return of 10.0 percent when I can safely get 12.0 percent by investing in Treasury bills?" Again, the misconception can be cleared up by explaining that the 10.0 percent return of common stocks was achieved during a time period when Treasury bills were returning 3.5 percent in an average inflationary environment of 3.1 percent. Based on the model we developed for common stock returns, in an environment where Treasury bills are yielding 12.0 percent, we would expect common stocks to provide an incremental compound return of 6.5 percent, or a total return of approximately 18.5 percent.

APPENDIX: STATISTICAL CONCEPTS

The first column of numbers in Table 3-1 is the "Geometric Mean," which is another expression for compound annual return. The "Arithmetic Mean" shown in the second column refers to the simple average of the returns in the series. An example will illustrate the difference. Assume we invest $100 in a stock, which during the first year increases in value to $125, for a total return of +25 percent. During the second year, the stock has a total return of −20 percent, decreasing in value from $125 back to the original $100. The arithmetic mean of these two annual returns is the sum of these two numbers divided by two:

Year 1 return	$= +\ 25\%$
Year 2 return	$= -\ 20\%$
Sum	$= +\ \ \ 5\%$
Arithmetic Mean $=$ Sum/2	$=\ \ \ \ 2.5\%$

The geometric mean (compound annual return), however, is 0 percent (i.e., a $100 investment that is worth $100 two years later has a geometric mean of 0 percent). For any series of numbers, the arithmetic mean will always be greater than or equal to the geometric mean. The difference between the arithmetic and geometric means is larger for a series of highly variable numbers. Only in the situation where the numbers in a series are constant will the arithmetic and geometric means be equal. The disparity between these two measures arises from the fact that it takes a larger percentage gain to offset a given percentage loss.

The arithmetic mean is the appropriate measure of typical performance for a single time period. The geometric mean is more appropriate when one is comparing returns over multiple time periods, as it represents the growth rate for an investment that is continually compounded. Often models that describe the expected return for various investment alternatives are single-period models, which accordingly incorporate terms using arithmetic means. Because the purpose of this book is to develop a framework for establishing long-term (i.e., multiple-period) investment policies, the comparison of relative historical performance and models of future expected performance will utilize geometric means (compound annual returns).

Throughout this book, in order to derive a risk premium or inflation-adjusted return, the geometric return of one investment alternative has been *arithmetically* subtracted from another, or from inflation. For example, common stocks' geometric mean of 10.0 percent was subtracted from Treasury bills' geometric mean of 3.5 percent to derive the equity risk premium of 6.5 percent. Ibbotson Associates, who provided the historical data on Treasury bills, bonds, and stock returns used in this book, prefers to state risk premiums and inflation-adjusted returns as the geometric differences between various return series. For example, the geometric difference between 7.0 percent and 13.0 percent is not 6.0 percent but 5.6 percent, computed as follows:

$$\frac{(1.13)}{(1.07)} - 1 = 5.6\%$$

The models developed in this book are to be used to provide a *conceptual* understanding of investment performance for both adviser and *client*. For this reason, in developing models the arithmetic difference rather than the geometric difference has been used in order to be consistent with the way a client typically thinks. (Most people think of the difference between 7.0 percent and 13.0 percent as being 6.0 percent, not 5.6 percent.) This simpler approach does not impair the conceptual value of the model and avoids getting side-tracked in explanations of geometric versus arithmetic differences.

The "expected return" of an investment is calculated as the weighted average of its possible returns, where the weights are the corresponding probability for each return.

Thus, both the value of each outcome, and its probability of occurrence, are incorporated into this single statistic.

For example, Figure 3-3 describes an investment in common stock XYZ which, depending on three alternative economic scenarios, will have a return of either −5.0 percent, 10.0 percent, or 25.0 percent. We can express the probability of each economic scenario in decimal form. For example, scenario A has a 25.0 percent likelihood of occurrence and is therefore assigned a probability of .25. Table 3-2 shows the mathematics for calculating the 10.75 percent expected return from an investment in common stock XYZ.

Alternative investments vary in terms of their expected returns, but an investment's expected return is only one aspect of future performance. It is equally important to simultaneously consider the risk of an investment. The more widely an investment's return may vary from its expected return, the more risky it is. The "standard deviation" is a commonly used measure of this variability. To calculate the standard deviation, deviations are derived by subtracting

FIGURE 3-3
Probability of Various Returns from an Investment in Common Stock XYZ

TABLE 3-2
Calculating the Expected Return for Common Stock XYZ

(1)	(2)	(3)	(4) = (2) × (3)
Economic Scenario	Probability of Occurrence	Return	Calculation of Expected Return
A	.25	−5%	−1.25%
B	.45	10	4.50
C	.30	25	7.50
	1.00		10.75% = Expected Return

the expected return from each possible return. These deviations are then squared and multiplied by their corresponding probabilities before being added together. The resulting sum is the variance (or probability weighted average squared deviation). The square root of the variance is the standard deviation. In our example, the standard deviation of return is 11.1 and is calculated as shown in Table 3-3.

In the real world, the possible returns from an investment cannot usually be divided into three discrete possibilities as in our example. Rather, the range of possible returns forms a continuous curve or "probability distribution," similar to that shown in Figure 3-4. Because the distribution of returns is continuous, probabilities are described for various ranges of outcomes. For example, the probability that the return from common stock ABC will fall between 5 percent and 10 percent can be determined by calculating what portion of the total area under the curve lies between 5 percent and 10 percent on the horizontal axis. If, for example, the blackened area represents 9 percent of the area underneath the curve, then there is a 9 percent likelihood (or .09 probability) that the return from common stock ABC will fall between 5 percent and 10 percent.

The probability distribution shown in Figure 3-4 is the familiar bell-shaped curve or "normal distribution." A normal distribution has attractive statistical properties. For example, it can be completely specified by using only two

TABLE 3-3
Calculating the Standard Deviation of Returns for Common Stock XYZ

(1) Economic Scenario	(2) Probability of Occurrence	(3) Return	(4) = (3) − 10.75% Deviation	(5) = (4)² Deviation Squared	(6) = (2) × (5) Probability Times Deviation Squared
A	.25	−5%	−15.75%	248.06	62.02
B	.45	10	−.75	.56	.25
C	.30	25	14.25	203.06	60.92
				Variance =	123.19
			Standard Deviation = Square root of variance =		11.10

FIGURE 3–4
Probability of Various Returns from an Investment in Common Stock ABC

Time Horizon: 1
Required Return: 0.00%

10%

5%

-50.0   -24.0   2.0   28.0   54.0   80.0
ANNUAL RATE OF RETURN

Source: Figure produced using Vestek Systems, Inc. software.

numbers: the mean and the standard deviation. That is, given only these two numbers, anyone would draw the same bell-shaped curve. The curve is symmetrically centered on its mean with 68 percent (approximately two thirds) of the area underneath the curve lying within 1 standard deviation of the mean, and 95 percent lying within 2 standard deviations.

In the example in Figure 3-4, the mean is the expected return of 15 percent and the standard deviation of 20 percent is the measure of risk which describes the dispersion of possible returns around the expected return. Given the properties of a normal distribution, we therefore know that the chances are roughly 2 out of 3 (i.e., a probability of .68) that the realized return will be between −5 percent and +35 percent (i.e., 15 percent +/−20 percent) and the chances are roughly 95 out of 100 that the realized return will be between −25 percent and +55 percent (i.e., 15 percent +/−40 percent).

Often an assumption is made that certain components of security returns are normally distributed when they are actually better described by a lognormal distribution, which has a longer "right tail." This is because security returns often do not have an upside limit but nevertheless have a downside limit of −100 percent. For simplicity, we will assume normal rather than lognormal distributions, where appropriate.

The last column in Table 3-1 specifies "First-order Autocorrelations." The first-order autocorrelation, or serial correlation, describes the extent to which the return in one period is helpful in predicting the return in the following period. A series of returns with a first-order autocorrelation near 1.0, for example, would be highly predictable from one period to the next, and indicative of a trend. If the first-order autocorrelation is near −1.0, the series is highly cyclical. If the first-order autocorrelation is near 0, then the series has no predictable pattern and is described as a "random walk." The high values assigned for the income returns produced by stocks and bonds indicate that each follows a trend from year to year. The patterns of total returns from stocks and long-term bonds, however, more closely resemble random walks, as evidenced by their correspondingly low first-order autocorrelations. This is caused by the variability of the principal value which is characteristic of stocks and long-term bonds.

Although not shown in this exhibit, the first-order autocorrelation for the small stock premium is .38, which suggests that it tends to follow a trend. A review of the historical comparative performance of common stocks versus small company stocks confirms that there are often prolonged periods of time when one of these investment alternatives outperforms the other. For example, small company stocks lagged the performance of larger capitalization stocks significantly from the middle of 1983 through roughly the end of 1987.

Then, 1988 witnessed a resurgence of small company stocks while larger capitalization stocks lagged. Although it is too early to tell, the relatively high first-order autocorrelation for the small stock premium suggests that small stocks may continue to outperform large company stocks for an extended period.

CHAPTER 4

MARKET TIMING

The evidence on investment managers' success with market timing is impressive—and overwhelmingly negative.

> —*Charles D. Ellis* (1937-   )
> Investment Policy, 1985

He that cannot abide a bad market, deserves not a good one.

> —*John Ray* (1627-1705)
> English Proverbs, 1678

Put all your eggs in one basket and—WATCH THAT BASKET.

> —*Mark Twain* (1935-1910)
> Pudd'nhead Wilson, 1894

The nightingale which cannot bear the thorn
It is best that it should never speak of the rose.

> —*Anwar-i-Suhaili*
> The Lights of Canopus

Common stocks have volatile returns. One consequence of that volatility is that investors have historically suffered negative annual returns approximately 30 percent of the time. Obviously, if there were a way to avoid the stock market's bad years, wealth would accumulate much more rapidly. Assume, for example, that it is December 31, 1925, and we are consulting a market timer who has made forecasts of 1926 security returns for Treasury bills, long-term government bonds, long-term corporate bonds, common stocks, and small stocks. He correctly predicts that of these five investment alternatives, common stocks will produce the best total return for 1926. We invest $1.00, which by the end of 1926 grows to be worth $1.12. Impressed with our market timer's predictive abilities, we again meet with him on December 31, 1926, for his advice as to where to position our money for the following year. Year after year our market timer, with perfect predictive accuracy, advises us concerning which investment alternative is appropriate for our market-timed portfolio.

Through compounding our wealth in this manner, our initial $1.00 investment would have grown to be worth approximately $2,650,000 by the end of 1988. This compares very favorably with the best-performing investment alternative, small stocks, with its ending value of $1,478, and with the more modest ending value of approximately $9 for Treasury bills! To contextualize this phenomenal result, consider the outcome had $1 million been initially invested at the end of 1925. By the end of 1988, the portfolio would have been worth $2.65 trillion—slightly more than the market value of all outstanding shares of all publicly traded common stocks in the United States. In essence, our 1925 millionaire would now own substantially all of corporate America!

Clearly, such market timing ability does not exist. Why then the persistent interest in market timing? People want to believe it is possible. Its appeal is truly seductive. When clients look at the long-term historical performance of common stocks, the hope of market timing is reinforced by what appears to be predictive trends—sustained periods of either rising or falling prices.[1] The resolution of this seeming contradiction lies in the recognition that a random series of numbers does not always look random! A simple experiment

---

[1]Despite appearances to the contrary, common stock returns do not follow a trend. This is indicated in Table 3-1 which shows that the first-order autocorrelation for common stock returns is .01.

will verify this. Take a coin, flip it 100 times and record the pattern of heads and tails produced. As you reach the end of the experiment, you will quite likely notice occasional runs of heads or runs of tails. Your knowledge of the nature of the coin flipping process prevents you, however, from inappropriately presuming the existence of predictive trends of either heads or tails. Each flip is independent of the preceding one.

When we examine the pattern of returns for common stocks, we see the same phenomenon. The run of heads in our coin flipping experiment becomes a prolonged period of rising stock market prices, classified as a bull market. The run of tails corresponds to the bear market. As we experience a prolonged bear market, such as occurred in 1973-1974, we tend to punish ourselves after the fact by concluding that we should have known that the bear market would have continued once prices started falling. This is particularly true in the midst of a bear market, when the public is reminded day by day in the financial press and on the evening news about how foolish it is to own common stocks. Similarly, common stock prices bottomed out during the summer of 1982, prior to one of the biggest bull markets in history. With the benefit of retrospect, people tend to conclude that everyone should have known that stocks were cheap during the summer of 1982 and poised for a big rise. The fact is that investors, in the aggregate, did not know stocks were a great bargain, otherwise their prior buying activity would have prevented the stocks from becoming such bargains in the first place. On the eve of this bull market, the financial press was filled with gloom and doom, with only an occasional voice crying in the wilderness regarding outstanding stock values.

An efficient market incorporates into current security prices relevant known information, as well as consensus expectations regarding the unknown. Thus, when it comes to predicting stock market movements, it is not of any value to know whether we are at war or peace, have a Republican or Democrat in the White House, or have been in an economic expansion or contraction. What then moves the market? It is measured by new information relevant to the pricing of investments, which was not previously known. In essence, it is the surprises that no one sees coming which trigger price movements to establish new equilibriums in the markets. These surprises themselves are random events. Occasionally there are more good surprises than bad, and we have a bull market. Other times the reverse is true, and we have a bear market. There will always be bulls and bears, but the evidence indicates that there is no consistent way to predict the turning points.

Before engaging in a review of the research studies on market timing, it is helpful to review some statistics on stock market cycles, as summarized in a research paper by Trinity Investment Management Corporation. The data covers the nine peak-to-peak cycles since World War II. The first cycle began May 29, 1946, and the last cycle ended August 25, 1987. Trinity observed:

1. There are about 1.7 times as many up months as down months: 309 versus 187.
2. The average bull market is up 104.8 percent versus the average bear market's drop of −28.0 percent.
3. Bull markets last nearly three times as long as bear markets: 41 months for the up legs versus 14 for the down legs.
4. Even within the bear markets, on average about 3 to 4 months out of 10 are up months.

Trinity makes the further observation that during bull markets, on average, only 8 months (out of the 41-month average bull market duration) accounted for more than 60 percent of the total return achieved.

Clearly, the average advance in a bull market is more than sufficient to regain the ground lost during a typical bear market. The fact that, in bear markets, 3 to 4 months out of 10 are up months reinforces the notion that it is often difficult to know that a bear market is occurring, until one is looking back after the fact. According to a research study by William F. Sharpe,

> . . . a manager who attempts to time the market must be right roughly three times out of four, merely to match the

overall performance of those competitors who don't. If he is right less often his relative performance will be inferior. There are two reasons for this. First, such a manager will often have his funds in cash equivalents in good market years, sacrificing the higher returns stocks provide in such years. Second, he will incur transaction costs in making switches, many of which will prove to be unprofitable.

Regarding the potential gains from market timing, Sharpe concluded that,

> Barring truly devastating market declines similar to those of The Depression, it seems likely that gains of little more than four percent per year from timing should be expected from a manager whose forecasts are truly prophetic.[2]

A study by Robert H. Jeffrey concluded:

> No one can predict the market's ups and downs over a long period, and the risks of trying outweigh the rewards.

He goes on to comment:

> The rationale for being a full-time equity investor is not that there are more positive real return periods than negative ones in most time frames, but rather that most of the "positive action" is compressed into just a few periods, which (perversely but understandably) tend to follow particularly adverse times for stocks.[3]

With reference to Ibbotson Associates' examination of security returns from 1926 through 1988, suppose that a common stock investor had missed the six best years for common stocks, during which time he alternatively had invested in Treasury bills. By being on the sidelines in cash equivalents during this critical 10 percent of the time period, $1 initially invested in stocks at the end of 1925 would have declined from what would have been $406 with continuous

---

[2]William F. Sharpe, "Likely Gains from Market Timing," *Financial Analysts Journal*, March–April, 1975, pp. 60–69.
[3]Robert H. Jeffrey, "The Folly of Stock Market Timing," *Harvard Business Review*, July–August, 1984, pp. 102–10.

investment in the S&P 500 to only $45 as a consequence of having missed these six superlative years.

Consider a market timer who has a 50/50 forecasting ability—that is, he is wrong in his predictions as often as he is right. Depending on which years he is wrong, his investment experience will vary widely. If he is lucky, he will be in the wrong place at the wrong time when the spread between Treasury bills and the S&P 500 is narrow, thereby not suffering significantly from the error. If, however, his mistakes more often than not occur during time periods when the spread is quite large, then the results can be disastrous. Based on the capital market experience 1926 through 1982, Jeffrey concluded:

> . . . if the theoreticians are correct about the inefficiency of market timing (that is, it will generally be accurate only 50% of the time), the probable outcome is a best-case real dollar return only about two times greater than what would come from continuous investment in the S&P, while the worst case produces about one hundred times less!
>
> The point of these . . . statistics is simply to emphasize that a market-timing strategist has tremendous natural odds to overcome, and that these odds increase geometrically with the length of the time frame and with the frequency of the timing interval. There is probably no situation where caveat emptor is more apropos for the portfolio owner than in interviewing prospective timing managers.[4]

Much of the problem with market timing concerns the fact that a disproportionate percentage of the total gain from a bull market tends to occur very rapidly at the beginning of a market recovery. If a market timer is on the sidelines in cash during this critical time, he is apt to miss too much of the action.

In another study, Jess S. Chua and Richard S. Woodward approached the subject from another angle in attempting to ascertain whether it is an inability to avoid bear markets or the tendency to miss the early part of a market recov-

---

[4]Jeffrey, "The Folly of Stock Market Timing," pp. 107–8.

ery that accounts for the poor results achieved from market timing. They concluded:

> Overall, the results show that it is more important to correctly forecast bull markets than bear markets. If the investor has only a 50% chance of correctly forecasting bull markets, then he should not practice market timing at all. His average return will be less than that of a buy-and-hold strategy even if he can forecast bear markets perfectly.

These researchers concluded that for market timing to pay:

> Investors require the forecast accuracies of at least:
> 80% bull and 50% bear;
> 70% bull and 80% bear; or
> 60% bull and 90% bear . . .[5]

This is particularly interesting because professional market timers most often stress capital preservation and the ability to avoid bear markets as the major benefit to be derived from their services.

In his wonderful book, *Investment Policy*,[6] Charles D. Ellis referred to an unpublished study of 100 large pension funds:

> . . . their experience with market timing found that while all the funds had engaged in at least some market timing, not one of the funds had improved its rate of return as a result of its efforts at timing. In fact, 89 of the 100 lost as a result of "timing"—and their losses averaged a daunting 4.5 percent over the five-year period.

Although long-term gains from market timing are highly unlikely, there will always be investors who have positive results from timing activities—particularly in the

---

[5]Jess H. Chua and Richard S. Woodward, *Gains from Stock Market Timing,* Monograph 1986-2 of *Monograph Series in Finance and Economics,* ed. Anthony Saunders (New York: Salomon Brothers Center for the Study of Financial Institutions at the Graduate School of Business Administration of New York University), pp. 12–13.

[6]Charles D. Ellis, *Investment Policy* (Homewood, Ill.: Dow Jones-Irwin, 1985), p. 13.

short-run. This is because over any single period, there will be a wide dispersion of investor experiences, with some investors doing well and some doing very poorly. Statistically, this is what we expect. The danger is the leap of logic which presumes that the good market timing result is caused by superior predictive ability. In the aggregate, market timing does not work, and most investor experiences have been and will be negative. Those market timers who have most recently made the right moves, however, are written up in financial publications and interviewed on television. This fuels the hopes of those who wish there were a way to get the advantage of a bull market while avoiding the pain of a bear market. Meanwhile, unsuccessful market timing firms fade away as clients reallocate what is left of their portfolios to the newly identified market timing guru. Many investors prefer to live with false hope, rather than critically examine whether market timing is possible at all. As Aristotle observed: "A plausible impossibility is always preferable to an unconvincing possibility." To face the question of whether market timing is possible forces an investor to acknowledge that he may have to either periodically face the pain of a bear market, or alternatively forego investing in common stocks altogether and thereby sacrifice the possibility of real capital growth. There is a pervasive human tendency to reinterpret one's experience to fit preconceptions. This is often the case with market timing, where hope springs eternal that somewhere, someone will somehow be able to consistently catch the bull while safely avoiding the bear.

The alternative to market timing is to simply buy and hold common stocks. As William Sharpe points out:

> A manager who keeps assets in stocks at all times is like an optimistic market timer. His actions are consistent with a policy of predicting a good year every year. While such a manager may know that such predictions will be wrong roughly one year out of three, such an attitude is nonetheless likely to lead to results superior to those achieved by most market timers.[7]

---

[7]Sharpe, "Likely Gains from Stock Market Timing," p. 67.

This chapter opens with a quote from Charles D. Ellis, and I would like to close the discussion with another of his observations:

> In investment management, the real opportunity to achieve superior results is not in scrambling to outperform the market, but in establishing *and adhering to* appropriate investment policies over the long term—policies that position the portfolio to benefit from riding with the main long-term forces in the market.[8]

---

[8]Ellis, *Investment Policy*, pp. 22-23.

CHAPTER 5

TIME HORIZON

He who wishes to be rich in a day will be hanged
in a year.
>—*Leonardo da Vinci* (1452-1519)
>Notebooks, circa 1500

Money is of a prolific generating nature. Money can
beget money, and its offspring can beget more.
>—*Benjamin Franklin* (1706-1790)
>Letters: To My Friend, A. B., 1748

Time is Archimedes' lever in investing.
>—*Charles D. Ellis* (1937-   )
>Investment Policy, 1985

Consider for a moment all the investment alternatives we have reviewed thus far. If you were charged with the task of dividing these investment alternatives into two groups on the basis of their investment characteristics, how would you do it? One way would be to rank them on the basis of their historical returns and look for a natural dividing line. With reference to the information in Table 3-1, we see that the biggest gap in historical returns exists between corporate bonds and common stocks. Using this as our dividing line, we would find that one group of investments would consist of Treasury bills, intermediate-term government bonds, long-term government bonds, and long-term corporate bonds—all of the interest-generating alternatives.

The second group would consist of common stocks and small stocks—the equity alternatives with high historical returns. If we alternatively approached the task by ranking the investment alternatives on the basis of risk as measured by their historical volatilities, we would draw the natural dividing line in exactly the same place: between interest-generating investments and equity investments. Let us now contrast the investment characteristics of these two broad groupings.

An interest-generating investment is a loan that provides a return in the form of interest payments, with the promise that the principal will be returned at a stated maturity date. The primary advantage of this kind of investment is that the cash flows (interest payments and principal return) are specified in advance. The major disadvantage is that these investments tend to be very susceptible to inflation. Historically, interest-generating alternatives have not been capable of simultaneously producing an income stream while maintaining purchasing power.

By comparison, common stocks and small stocks are equity ownership interests in businesses. An equity investment provides return in the form of dividends and/or capital appreciation. It does not have a stated maturity nor is there any promise that the principal will be returned some day. But it also has no upper limit on its return possibilities. The primary advantage of an equity investment is the prospect for real (i.e., inflation adjusted) long-term capital growth. The major disadvantage of an equity investment is the high short-run volatility of principal value.

In essence, these two broad categories, interest-generating investments and equity investments, represent the two alternative ways of putting money to work. It is the traditional distinction of either being a "loaner or an owner." A low return is the price paid by the "loaner" who wants the advantage of a more predictable outcome. Short-run volatility of principal is the price paid by the "owner" who wants the long-term capital growth possible with equities. This is simply an acknowledgment of the risk/return relationship among investment alternatives. We previously discussed a wide variety of risks. In my opinion, however, the two most important money management risks are:

1. Inflation—which is most damaging to interest-generating investments.
2. Volatility—which is most pronounced with equity investments.

To focus our discussion, let us consider using Treasury bills as a proxy for interest-generating investments, and the S&P 500 common stock index as a proxy for equity investments. In summary:

	Treasury Bills	*S&P 500*
Advantage	Stability of principal value	Long-term real capital growth
Disadvantage	Susceptibility to inflation	Volatile returns

Given the higher returns produced by equity investments one could conclude that investors have greater fear of stock market volatility than they have of inflation. This is evidenced by the lower returns they willingly accept with Treasury bills in order to have stable principal values. In the aggregate, investors are overconcerned with the volatility of common stock returns and underconcerned regarding the damaging effects of inflation. There are several reasons for this. First, inflation is insidious, taking its toll little by little over the long term.

Second, investors who are not sensitive to the impact of inflation over time tend to view their investment results in nominal terms and generally prefer interest-generating alternatives. For example, during 1979 and 1980 when inflation reached a peak of 12 percent to 13 percent, Treasury bill returns were at a historical high of 10 percent to 11 percent. Treasury bill investors tended to look at the accumulation of interest, ignoring that these high nominal returns were insufficient to compensate for the impact of inflation. Many investors still look at 1979 and 1980 as "the good old days" of high money market returns and deplore the lower single-digit returns available as interest rates fell through the 1980s. Yet, these investors were actually much better off in the lower interest rate environment. Returns were much higher in *real* terms then than prevailed during 1979 and 1980. It would be interesting to see how perceptions would change if Treasury bill investors had their returns routinely reported to them in inflation adjusted terms.

Third, common stock volatility by comparison can do much more damage in the short-run. On October 19, 1987, for example, we saw common stocks drop more than 20 percent *in one day*, compared with the highest recent *annual* inflation rate of 13 percent in 1979. Unfortunately, many investors focus too narrowly on the short term, and incorrectly conclude that common stock losses are permanent. Some investors who suffered through the 1973–1974 bear market for common stocks sold their equities before participating in one of the best bull markets in this century. In their discouragement they said to themselves, "Common stocks?—never again!"

In the short-run, the possible negative consequences of stock market volatility will be much greater than the damage possible from inflation. Is the fear of common stock volatility warranted? In some circumstances it is, and in other situations, perhaps not. As we look into the future, there are two things we can count on. First, common stock returns will remain unpredictable and volatile. Second, people will prefer predictability over uncertainty. For example, consider a choice between the following investment alternatives. Investment A has an expected return of 8 percent, with a standard deviation of 1 percent. Investment B has an expected return of 8 percent, with a standard deviation of 5 percent. Both investments offer the same expected return, but investment B has five times the risk of investment A. Rational investors are risk-averse. Given these alternatives, such investors will choose investment A. There is no incentive for bearing the risk of investment B. Economists refer to the "declining marginal utility of wealth" as underlying the explanation for this risk aversion. That is, each additional dollar that is acquired always increases one's well-being, but it does so at a declining rate. An extra 100 dollars means more to you if your net worth is 1,000 dollars, than if you are a millionaire. In an investment context, this means that the additional dollar you make with a good outcome is not as valuable as the dollar that is lost with a bad outcome. In the real world, investors would sell investment B to buy investment A. By their doing so, the price of A would rise and the price of B would fall. In equilibrium, investment B would have a higher expected return to compensate for its greater risk.

The same is true in our comparison of Treasury bills and common stocks. The buying and selling activities of investors in the marketplace cause stocks to be priced to provide higher expected returns than Treasury bills, as compensation for bearing the risk of equities.

In the last chapter we presented evidence that indicated that market timing does not work. Consider what would happen, however, if there were an easy way to time the stock market. Investors would buy stocks in advance of a market rise and sell them in advance of a foreseen decline. This buying and selling activity, however, would change the pattern of future stock price behavior by smoothing out the market's ups and downs. There is only one problem: When common stock volatility disappears so does the reward for bearing it! I therefore *prefer* a world where common stocks retain their short-run unpredictable volatility. It is the foundation upon which common stocks' long-term higher returns are built. Implicit in the market timer's world view is the notion that money is made in common stocks *despite* the risk. In contrast, the world view presented here rests on the notion that money is made in common stocks *because* of the risk. Now, the question becomes, "Under what conditions is the risk worth assuming?" If we allocate the 6.5 percent equity risk premium across each of the 365 days in the year, we would find that the daily performance advantage of common stocks relative to Treasury bills practically disappears. On any given day, the chances are basically 50/50 that common stocks will outperform Treasury bills. Given the ever present volatility of common stocks, there is no incentive to assume equity risk on the basis of a one-day time horizon. The same is true for one-month and one-year investments in common stocks. The standard deviation of common stocks has historically been 20.9 percent. (Refer to Table 3-1.) This is much larger than the equity risk premium we expect to receive on average from holding common stocks. In the short-run, although we expect to have higher returns in common stocks, the high volatility will swamp recognition of the equity risk premium. This is particularly troublesome for unsophisticated investors who often confuse this volatility for evidence of an irrational marketplace.

Time is one of the most important dimensions of the money management process. It is also often the least understood by investors. In assessing investment alternatives, time horizon determines appropriateness. If it is known that an investor will need $20,000 next month to buy a car, a money market fund is a reasonable investment in the interim. A pension plan with known future nominal obligations (i.e., there's no provision for inflation adjusted benefits) may decide to match the duration of those obligations with similar duration bonds or follow an immunization strategy. Most longer term investment situations, however, do not involve objectives with specific future nominal needs. There is simply too much uncertainty in the direction and magnitude of inflation. More often, the goal is therefore the preservation and/or accumulation of wealth in real terms. This requires the utilization of equity investments. Whereas in the short-run, we concluded that the risk of equities is too great relative to the expected reward, this changes as the time horizon lengthens. For example, based on Ibbotson Associates' capital market data from 1926 through 1988, common stocks outperformed Treasury bills in 39 of the 63 years, or 62 percent of the time. If we compare the performance over longer holding periods of 5 years, 10 years, and 20 years, however, we find that common stocks increasingly dominate Treasury bills 78 percent, 81 percent, and finally, 100 percent of the time, respectively.

Assume for a moment that we have a stable inflation

and interest rate environment. As the time horizon time lengthens, the expected return from common stocks will not change, but the variability of holding-period compound returns will decline dramatically. The longer the holding period, the more opportunity there is for good years to offset bad years, with the result that the range of average returns converges on the expected return. In Table 5-1, for example, comparisons are made among compound returns for common stocks, corporate bonds, government bonds, Treasury bills, and inflation for 1-, 5-, 10-, and 25-year holding periods. In examining the information for one-year holding periods, we see that in 37 of the 63 years (59 percent of the time) common stocks outperformed the three other investment alternatives. But, the returns ranged from −43.3 percent to 54.0 percent. Hence, although we expect stocks to outperform other investment alternatives in any given year, the penalty for being wrong can be quite high. The ranges of returns for other investment alternatives are narrower as expected, given their lower standard deviations.

As we stretch the time horizon to 10 years, common stocks now dominate the other investment alternatives in 41 out of 54 periods, or 76 percent of the time. Not only has our confidence in being right with common stocks increased, but the penalty for a bad outcome moreover is considerably less. The worst 10-year common stock experience produced a compound average return of −.9 percent. On that basis, a $10,000 investment would have declined to $9,136 with full reinvestment of income. In 98 percent of the 10-year holding periods, the outcome was better than that! Finally, we see that with 25-year holding periods, common stocks dominated the three other investment alternatives 100 percent of the time. It is quite interesting to see that the worst 25-year compound return for common stocks of 5.9 percent was almost as good as the very best 25-year compound returns of 6.7 percent, 6.2 percent, and 6.9 percent for corporate bonds, government bonds, and Treasury bills, respectively. The volatility of common stocks is undoubtedly an enemy in the short-run. But it is the basis for common stocks' higher expected return.

TABLE 5–1
Comparison of Investment Results for Various Holding Periods (1926 through 1988)

	Common Stocks	Corporate Bonds	Long-term Government Bonds	Treasury Bills	CPI
63 One-year Holding Periods					
Highest annual percent return	54.0	43.8	40.3	14.7	18.2
Lowest annual percent return	–43.3	–8.1	–9.2	0.0	–10.3
Number of periods with negative returns	19	15	18	1	10
Number of periods outpacing inflation	42	39	36	38	N.A.
Number of periods with best of four returns	37	10	6	10	N.A.
59 Five-year Holding Periods					
Highest compound annual percent return	23.9	22.4	21.6	11.1	10.1
Lowest compound annual percent return	–12.5	–2.2	–2.1	0.1	–5.4
Number of periods with negative compound returns	7	3	6	0	7
Number of periods outpacing inflation	45	31	28	33	N.A.
Number of periods with best of four returns	42	10	3	4	N.A.
54 Ten-year Holding Periods					
Highest compound annual percent return	20.1	10.9	10.6	9.2	8.7
Lowest compound annual percent return	–0.9	1.0	–0.1	0.1	–2.6
Number of periods with negative compound returns	2	0	1	0	6
Number of periods outpacing inflation	47	25	21	27	N.A.
Number of periods with best of four returns	41	7	0	6	N.A.
39 Twenty-five-year Holding Periods					
Highest compound annual percent return	14.7	6.7	6.2	6.9	5.6
Lowest compound annual percent return	5.9	1.5	1.2	0.6	1.3
Number of periods with negative compound returns	0	0	0	0	0
Number of periods outpacing inflation	39	17	10	18	N.A.
Number of periods with best of four returns	39	0	0	0	N.A.

Source: Based on data from Roger G. Ibbotson and Rex A. Sinquefield, *Stocks, Bonds, Bills, and Inflation* (SBBI), 1982, updated in *SBBI 1989 Yearbook*, Ibbotson Associates, Chicago.

Time transforms this short-run enemy into a friend for the long-term investor.

With Table 5-1 we noted that an investor's performance results will vary depending on the calendar year with which his holding period begins. Few clients, however, establish an investment position exactly at the beginning of a calendar year. The utilization of annual return data understates the range of returns for various holding periods. By changing the beginning point for various holding periods to a monthly rather than a calendar-year basis, Figure 5-1 provides a more comprehensive comparison of the range of returns for Treasury bills versus common stocks. The graph utilizes data from 1926 through 1988 and compares the range of returns for holding periods of 12 months (1 year) to 240 months (20 years). Observe the potentially high penalty for being in common stocks for holding periods as short as 12 months to 60 months. As the holding period lengthens, however, the range of compound annual returns converges dramatically. Note that *all* 240-month holding periods had positive compound annual returns. It is also quite interesting to observe that the median return for common stocks was approximately the same across the 12-, 60-, 120-, and 240-month holding periods. The median return for Treasury bills was, of course, much lower than common stocks, but was similarly relatively constant.

Figures 5-2A and 5-2B communicate the same message in a different form. Here, we can directly compare relative returns in a contemporaneous way for various holding periods. Again, we see that if stock market volatility is the disease, time is the cure.

The "miracle of compound interest" is also at work in the pattern of the increasing dominance of common stocks over time. What seems like a modest 6.5 percent equity risk premium produces hugh differences in wealth accumulation over long time periods. During the period 1926 through 1988, the 6.5 percent incremental return with common stocks produced more than 45 times the wealth accumulation of Treasury bills. Assume Treasury bills are now at 7.0 percent with

FIGURE 5-1
Common Stocks versus Treasury Bills. Range of Compound Annual Returns for Various Holding Periods (1926–1988)

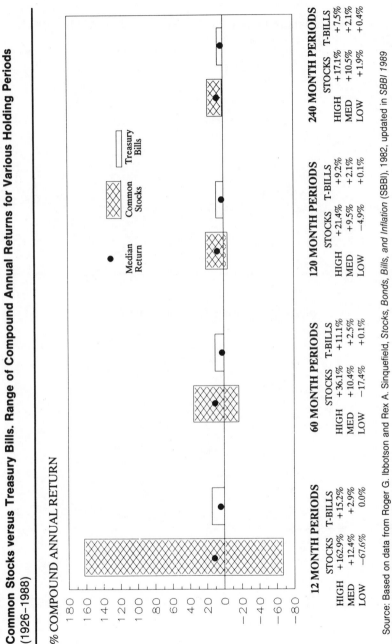

Source: Based on data from Roger G. Ibbotson and Rex A. Sinquefield, *Stocks, Bonds, Bills, and Inflation* (SBBI), 1982, updated in *SBBI 1989 Yearbook*, Ibbotson Associates, Chicago.

FIGURE 5-2A
Common Stocks versus Treasury Bills. Compound Annual Returns for
Various Holding Periods (1926–1988)

ONE YEAR PERIODS ENDING

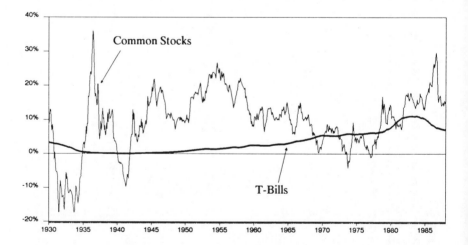

FIVE YEAR PERIODS ENDING

Source: Based on data from Roger G. Ibbotson and Rex A. Sinquefield, *Stocks, Bonds, Bills, and Inflation*
(SBBI), 1982, updated in *SBBI 1989 Yearbook*, Ibbotson Associates, Chicago.

FIGURE 5-2B
Common Stocks versus Treasury Bills. Compound Annual Returns for Various Holding Periods (1926–1988)

TEN YEAR PERIODS ENDING

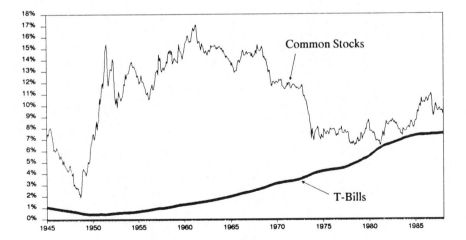

TWENTY YEAR PERIODS ENDING

Source: Roger G. Ibbotson and Rex A. Sinquefield, *Stocks, Bonds, Bills, and Inflation* (SBBI), 1982, updated in *SBBI 1989 Yearbook*, Ibbotson Associates, Chicago.

the corresponding expected return for common stocks at 13.0 percent. With reference to Table 5-2, we see that in only 13 years the cumulative wealth from an investment in common stocks would double that of a corresponding investment in Treasury bills. By 20 years, common stocks would be worth nearly 3 times that of an investment in Treasury bills.

In summary, volatility swamps the expected payoff from common stocks in the short-run, making them a risk not worth taking. But, in the long-run, common stocks emerge as the winner, because of the convergence of average returns around common stocks' higher expected return, coupled with the miracle of compounding interest.

TABLE 5-2
Growth of $1 at Interest

Years	6%	7%	8%	9%	10%	11%	12%	13%	14%
1	1.06	1.07	1.08	1.09	1.10	1.11	1.12	1.13	1.14
2	1.12	1.14	1.17	1.19	1.21	1.23	1.25	1.28	1.30
3	1.19	1.23	1.26	1.30	1.33	1.37	1.40	1.44	1.48
4	1.26	1.31	1.36	1.41	1.46	1.52	1.57	1.63	1.69
5	1.34	1.40	1.47	1.54	1.61	1.69	1.76	1.84	1.93
6	1.42	1.50	1.59	1.68	1.77	1.87	1.97	2.08	2.19
7	1.50	1.61	1.71	1.83	1.95	2.08	2.21	2.35	2.50
8	1.59	1.72	1.85	1.99	2.14	2.30	2.48	2.66	2.85
9	1.69	1.84	2.00	2.17	2.36	2.56	2.77	3.00	3.25
10	1.79	1.97	2.16	2.37	2.59	2.84	3.11	3.39	3.71
11	1.90	2.10	2.33	2.58	2.85	3.15	3.48	3.84	4.23
12	2.01	2.25	2.52	2.81	3.14	3.50	3.90	4.33	4.82
13	2.13	2.41	2.72	3.07	3.45	3.88	4.36	4.90	5.49
14	2.26	2.58	2.94	3.34	3.80	4.31	4.89	5.53	6.26
15	2.40	2.76	3.17	3.64	4.18	4.78	5.47	6.25	7.14
16	2.54	2.95	3.43	3.97	4.59	5.31	6.13	7.07	8.14
17	2.69	3.16	3.70	4.33	5.05	5.90	6.87	7.99	9.28
18	2.85	3.38	4.00	4.72	5.56	6.54	7.69	9.02	10.58
19	3.03	3.62	4.32	5.14	6.12	7.26	8.61	10.20	12.06
20	3.21	3.87	4.66	5.60	6.73	8.06	9.65	11.52	13.74
21	3.40	4.14	5.03	6.11	7.40	8.95	10.80	13.02	15.67
22	3.60	4.43	5.44	6.66	8.14	9.93	12.10	14.71	17.86
23	3.82	4.74	5.87	7.26	8.95	11.03	13.55	16.63	20.36
24	4.05	5.07	6.34	7.91	9.85	12.24	15.18	18.79	23.21
25	4.29	5.43	6.85	8.62	10.83	13.59	17.00	21.23	26.46

Time horizon is the key variable in determining the appropriate balance of interest-generating versus equity investments in a portfolio. This is summarized in the following comparison:

	Treasury Bills	Common Stocks
Major Risk	Inflation	Short-run volatility
Primary Advantage	Principal stability	Long-term growth
Appropriate for	Short time horizons	Long time horizons

Investors generally tend to underestimate their relevant time horizons. For example, consider new clients, husband and wife, both age 60, who when discussing their time horizon comment: "We both work now, but want to retire at age 65. Because we are only 5 years from retirement, our time horizon is very short. Equities were fine when we were young and building assets for retirement. But now that retirement is approaching, we should be cashing out of stocks to move into certificates of deposit and bonds, so that we can use the interest for living expenses during retirement."

This couple has confused their retirement horizon with their investment portfolio time horizon. The latter is *much* longer. If they plan to rely on their portfolio to support them through retirement, then their time horizon extends until the death of the survivor of them. For a man and woman of average health, both age 60, the life expectancy of the survivor of them is more than 25 years. As we have seen, during a 25-year time horizon, the dangers of inflation are greater than the risks of common stock volatility, and accordingly, equities should be meaningfully represented in their portfolio.

The tendency for investors to underestimate their time horizons leads to portfolios that are inappropriately underweighted in equities and therefore overexposed to inflation. This tendency is reinforced by the client's desire to measure performance over quarterly and annual time periods. Such measurement intervals are much too short to get a realistic assessment of progress toward the achievement of long-term objectives.

A proper understanding of time horizon as it relates to the investment process can dramatically alter a person's risk tolerance. The next chapter builds a simple model for guiding clients in making the most important decision impacting portfolio performance: the balance between interest-generating versus equity investments.

CHAPTER 6

A MODEL FOR DETERMINING BROAD PORTFOLIO BALANCE

Everything should be made as simple as possible, but not simpler.

—*Albert Einstein* (1879–1955)

The client-adviser relationship begins with the "Data-Gathering Session." The purpose of this process is to get to know the client. Much of the information solicited is factual in nature and can be objectively determined. For personal clients, this information includes the value of assets and liabilities, sources of income and expenditures, tax situation, family composition, employment information, etc. For small institutional clients, such as qualified retirement plans or endowments, this information includes a list of investment positions, anticipated contributions and withdrawals from the portfolio, and a description of legal or regulatory constraints.

Another area of data gathering is subjective in nature and requires a more qualitative approach. This is the realm of client psychology, hopes and dreams, opinions and preferences regarding investments, and tolerance for various types of risk. Specifically, let us discuss the challenges involved in assessing the client's:

1. Specific goals.
2. Investment objectives.
3. Investment knowledge.
4. Risk tolerance.

SPECIFIC GOALS

Examples of goals for a personal money management client include:

1. Early retirement.
2. College education for children.
3. Buying a vacation home.
4. Providing for an aging parent with declining health.

For small institutional money management clients the goals might be to:

1. Provide retirement benefits to participants in a qualified plan.
2. Fund the charitable pursuits of an endowment fund.

When these goals are expressed, they often lack specificity. The adviser needs to help the client flesh out the goals in more detail. For example, does early retirement mean age 50, age 55, or age 60? What lifestyle does the client want in retirement, and what level of income will be necessary to sustain it? If the client wants to send three children to college, will they attend high-priced private institutions, or less expensive public universities? Will scholarships be likely? Will the children get jobs to contribute to their own expenses? If the children are young, at what rate will tuitions rise in the interim? Is a vacation home purchase a short-term or long-term goal? Approximately what price range are they considering? What would be the expenses associated with a vacation home? Does the client anticipate renting it when it is not in use? What kind of rental income could be obtained? In the situation of the aging parent, is support presently being provided by the client? What sources of income does the parent presently have, and are there assets that can be sold to provide additional funds if needed? What kind of health insurance coverage does the parent have, and will he qualify for some form of government assistance for medical bills or income needs? Similarly, greater specificity can be developed for institutional clients who have quantifiable needs to fund future benefit payments.

INVESTMENT OBJECTIVES

Once the client goals have been specified, the next step is to develop investment objectives that correspond to those goals. Much of this can be described mathematically in a relatively straightforward manner. Subject to reasonable assumptions, for example, we can calculate the annual investment necessary at a specified growth rate to accumulate a predetermined future sum of money. Very often, however, client goals are more ambitious than can realistically be achieved. We have all had clients who decide to get serious about their retirement goals a few years prior to retirement. They are ready to modify their lifestyles as necessary to free up funds for investment in order to be assured a comfortable retirement. By that point, however, the lifestyle supportable at retirement has been largely determined. If the lifestyle is found to be seriously inadequate, there is probably little that can be done to materially improve it. Human desires tend to exceed the resources available to fund them. In developing investment objectives, goals must therefore be prioritized and often compromised in the process of determining what is realistically possible in any given situation. Sound investment objectives are built upon realistic capital market assumptions and reflect the limitations of the client's available income and resources.

INVESTMENT KNOWLEDGE

The best clients understand the general principles of money management and the characteristics of alternative investments. The long-term success of the investment management process depends to a large degree on the client's understanding of how his portfolio is structured and the manner in which it will behave. In the data-gathering process, it is helpful to have clients describe their good and bad experiences with investments. From their comments the breadth and depth of their knowledge can be gleaned. Often, advisers use questionnaires that exhaustively list many different

types of investment alternatives. Clients are asked to indicate their familiarity with, preference for, and prior use of
each investment alternative. I think it is important to recognize the primary purpose of such questionnaires and to be
aware of their limitations.

A client who indicates on a questionnaire familiarity with, preference for, and/or knowledge about common
stocks, for example, does not necessarily understand them
sufficiently to make informed decisions regarding their use.
At best, such questionnaires are a beginning point for an
educational process that meaningfully involves the client.
A significant danger exists in inappropriately using the re-
sponses to such questions as a basis for either inferring risk
tolerance or choosing building blocks for constructing a portfolio. A client who says he has never invested in bonds and
prefers not to use them, may be only expressing unfamiliar-
ity with them. It would be inappropriate to develop a portfolio excluding bonds solely on the basis of such a response.
By analogy, consider a person who consults a physician because of an ache or pain. The physician will not recommend
a course of treatment based on the patient's familiarity with
various prescription drugs. Investment preferences are often
based on incomplete or erroneous information and should
therefore not be used as the basis of a portfolio strategy or
assessment of risk tolerance.

RISK TOLERANCE

In investment management, risk is often equated with the
uncertainty (variability or standard deviation) of possible returns around the expected return. Clients, however, do not
typically think in terms of expected return and standard deviation. More often, clients think of risk as it is defined in the
dictionary: the chance of loss. Many investment counselors
are in agreement that it is more accurate to think of investors
as typically being "loss-averse" rather than "risk-averse."
For example, the variability of returns investors experience
from one year to another is not particularly troublesome so

long as there are no *negative* returns. Beneath the psychology of "loss aversion" lurks a conviction by some investors that negative returns represent permanent capital losses. Another problem with loss-aversion psychology is that clients tend to think in terms of nominal rather than real returns. For example, many investors would feel better about earning 5 percent after taxes in a 12 percent inflationary environment than they would about losing 1 percent after taxes in a 4 percent inflationary environment. The positive nominal gain of 5 percent in this example creates the illusion of getting ahead, although adjusted for the 12 percent inflation, there is a real loss of 7 percent. In actuality they would be better off losing 1 percent in the 4 percent inflationary environment for a smaller real loss of 5 percent. It would be interesting to see how investor perceptions and behavior would change if all investment returns were consistently reported in real rather than nominal returns.

Many clients are fearful of equity investments. In working with them, the task is not to convert them from "risk avoiders" to "risk takers." As we concluded earlier, it is very rational to be risk-averse. Simply put, there is greater pain in losing 100 dollars than there is satisfaction in gaining 100 dollars. Rather, the task is to sensitize the client to all the risks he faces, then to prioritize the relative dangers of these risks, *given the context of his situation.* This is why we explored in detail the impact time horizon has on the investment management process. Without guidance, most clients do not know how to realistically assess the risks they face. By default, they tend to assume that the familiar and comfortable path is the safe path, whereas anything unfamiliar or uncomfortable must be risky. For example, I have worked with a number of real estate professionals who consider themselves very risk-averse and fearful of common stocks. Yet, they are heavily invested in real estate (another equity) using high financial leverage. When the risk of such highly-leveraged equity investing is pointed out to them, the response is often: "There's no risk there. I *understand* real estate and am *comfortable* with it!"

Investment advisers use a variety of methods to assess

a client's ability to tolerate risk. For example, clients are asked to describe themselves as being either risk avoiders or risk takers. Another approach is to look for risk tolerance cues, based on the client's business and personal lifestyles. For example, a person who likes the security of working for one employer for a lifetime and prefers recreational horseshoes may be more risk-averse than a person who changes jobs relatively frequently in advancing his career, and likes to parachute on the weekends. The problems with these approaches are that they are highly subjective, and are difficult to translate into a measurement of investment risk tolerance. An examination of the client's current investment portfolio provides some clues but, again, the danger is that this may be more indicative of client familiarity and comfort with various investments than it is a measure of risk tolerance.

Whatever approach is used to assess risk tolerance, it is important to remember that it is not a fixed inherited characteristic like blue eyes that stay blue for the rest of one's life. Accordingly, it is dangerous to develop an investment strategy on the basis of an initial assessment of risk tolerance, regardless of how accurate the reading may be. To do so inappropriately presumes that a client already knows what is in his best interest. If the client's risk perceptions are inaccurate, he cannot make wise decisions. Our task is to provide a frame of reference that enables the client to correctly perceive risks within the context of his situation. Surprisingly, a client's risk tolerance can change within a rather broad range, based on an improved understanding of the investment management process. The informed modification of risk tolerance is one of our major responsibilities to our clients, and represents a great opportunity to add value. The modification of risk tolerance is often in the direction of helping clients to become more comfortable with equity investments for long time horizons. In other situations, however, clients may gain increased awareness that the incremental return expected from common stocks is not sufficient to compensate for the volatility of returns if the investment time horizon is short.

For these clients, risk tolerance is appropriately lowered with a corresponding reduction in equity investments as the client's perceptions become more realistic.

THE PORTFOLIO BALANCE MODEL

Admittedly, there is a gap between the money manager's world of "expected returns and standard deviations" and the client's world of "wanting to make lots of money without taking risks!" The first part of this book is devoted to a discussion of the long-term historical investment performance of various investment alternatives. On the basis of this information, we developed simple models to describe the expected returns and risks associated with these investment alternatives. As we steer the client through this capital market review, his perceptions and expectations become more realistic and his capacity is developed for making improved investment decisions. Without this process, few clients are equipped to make the right decisions for themselves. The most important decision that the client makes deals with the allocation of portfolio assets between interest-generating and equity investments. This decision determines the risk/return characteristics of the portfolio and quantifies both the likelihood of reaching his investment objectives and his risk in getting there. A methodology is needed which forces the client to deal realistically with the trade-off between risk and return. The model we will develop uses simplistic assumptions. Although some rigor may be lost in this simplicity, the effectiveness of the model should ultimately be judged by the criterion of whether it effectively helps the client to understand the risk/return trade-off. If the client makes better decisions and more confidently adheres to investment policies, the model accomplishes its purpose.

In Chapter 5, we divided the investment world into two categories—interest-generating investments and equity investments. We concluded that each category has a primary advantage and disadvantage. Interest-generating assets provide promises regarding payment of interest and principal, but are susceptible to purchasing power erosion as a consequence of inflation. By contrast, equity assets have historically been able to build purchasing power through capital growth, but have the disadvantage of short-run volatility. To highlight these differences, we chose Treasury bills as a proxy for interest-generating assets in general, and we chose common stocks, as represented by the S&P 500, as a proxy for the wide variety of equity investments. We concluded that the attractiveness of Treasury bills versus the S&P 500 was primarily determined by the investment time horizon. For long time horizons, inflation poses a larger risk than stock market volatility and accordingly, a portfolio should be oriented more heavily toward common stocks and other forms of equity investments. For short time horizons, stock market volatility is more dangerous than inflation, so portfolios should be more heavily positioned in Treasury bills and other interest-generating assets that have stable principal values.

By adding the long-term historical equity risk premium of 6.5 percent to the expected return of Treasury bills, we derived the expected return for common stocks. Given the high volatility of common stocks, we also know that the realized equity risk premium will vary widely. (Refer to Figure 3-1, which shows the historical volatility of the equity risk premium on a rolling five-year basis.) Unfortunately, the "real" equity risk premium is not subject to direct measurement. Some forecasters use macroeconomic models to try to predict the equity risk premium with greater accuracy. This, of course, presumes that the careful analysis and manipulation of macroeconomic data can provide a unique insight missed by the capital market participants as a whole—a very difficult achievement in highly efficient markets. Other forecasters evaluate the current economic environment and attempt to find similar conditions at other times in history to develop a better prediction of how the capital markets may behave. For example, if there is a concern regarding the prospects of accelerating inflation, historical returns are examined from other periods of history where accelerating inflation was experienced. This selective use of history presumes that we can correctly determine in retrospect what caused the markets to behave as they did, and that current market behavior will be determined by the same causal relationships. Again, this is quite difficult to do successfully.

The easy way out may also be the best way out. This is to simply assume that the historical equity risk premium of 6.5 percent is a reasonable estimate of what the equity risk premium should be. This has been the historical reward received for bearing equity risk, based on a long time horizon encompassing periods of both war and peace, economic expansions and contractions, high and low inflation, Republican and Democratic administrations, etc. There will always be unusual events, and arguably an estimate built on the basis of long-term experience may be the safest approach. The precision of this estimate of the equity risk premium is not particularly important for two reasons. First, in the short-run, the high standard deviation of common stock returns will always swamp recognition of the expected equity risk premium. So whether the "real" equity risk premium is 6 percent or 7 percent makes little difference. Second, the purpose of the methodology is not to derive accurate estimates of expected returns, but rather to develop a systematic way of making broad portfolio balance decisions that acknowledge the risk/return trade-off.

Let us discuss the steps involved in our methodology for guiding clients in making this most important investment policy decision impacting portfolio performance.

Step 1: *Verify that your client fully understands the risk/return characteristics of Treasury bills and common stocks (S&P 500).* Refer to Table 6–1.

Step 2: *Review with your client the importance of time horizon in assessing risks and evaluating appropriate investments.*

Step 3: *Determine the current value of your client's total investment portfolio.* This includes:

    A. All liquid and nonliquid investments (e.g., investment real estate) even though the latter cannot be easily converted to cash.

TABLE 6–1
Risk/Return Characteristics of Treasury Bills versus S&P 500

Expected Return	Volatility*	Comments
	Treasury Bills	
7%	±0%	The expected return of 7% is the yield on a one-year bill as shown in *The Wall Street Journal.* The volatility is shown as ±0% because the return can be locked in with no uncertainty.
	S&P 500	
13%	±21%	The expected return of 13% is derived by adding the historical equity risk premium of 6% (rounded to the nearest percentage) to the current Treasury bill yield of 7%. The volatility of ±21% is the historical standard deviation of returns for common stocks from 1926 through 1988.

*There are two chances out of three that the actual return will be in a range defined by the expected return plus or minus the volatility.

B. The value of employer-sponsored retirement plans. These are included even though the client may not have investment discretion of the funds.

C. The present value of annuitized streams of income. Although these are not normally thought of as investment assets and are seldom reflected on the balance sheet, they are nevertheless important economic assets that should be considered in structuring portfolios.

This third step helps the client to think of his portfolio in the broadest terms and focuses his attention on the "big picture."

Step 4: *Instruct your client to hypothetically convert this entire investment portfolio to cash. This conversion* overcomes inertia by freeing the client from the ghosts of his past investment decisions.

Step 5: *Describe a hypothetical investment world where there are only two investment alternatives— Treasury bills and the S&P 500*. Ask your client to allocate the cash from his liquidated investment portfolio between these two alternatives. In doing so, he should keep in mind the risk/return characteristics of each alternative and his relevant investment time horizon.

In reviewing the range of choices available to the client, consider a portfolio composed entirely of Treasury bills. Of all possible alternatives, this portfolio has the lowest expected return. This is the price paid for the elimination of uncertainty. As we begin to allocate money to the S&P 500, the risk of the resulting portfolio increases in direct proportion to the percentage invested in common stocks. Table 6–2 shows the risk/return characteristics of five portfolios ranging from 100 percent Treasury bills through 50 percent Treasury bills/50 percent S&P 500 to 100 percent invested in the S&P 500. Investment decisions are made under terms of uncertainty. For this reason, it is better to forecast portfolio results in terms of typical ranges around expected returns. For example, rather than simply saying portfolio 2 has an expected return of 9 percent, it is much more meaningful to indicate that the likelihood is two chances out of three that the actual result will be within plus or minus 7 percent of the expected return of 9 percent.

Clients bring to the client-adviser relationship their own expectations regarding the expected returns and risks associated with various investment alternatives. Often, clients believe that returns are more easily achieved with less risk than indicated here. Such clients struggle with the investment alternatives presented in Table 6–2. If so, that is good. If there is going to be a struggle over the nature of the risk/return trade-off, it is best to deal with it at this point in the process. Generally, clients will accept the framework

TABLE 6-2
Example Portfolio Choices

	Portfolio Balance		Expected Portfolio Performance		
	Treasury Bills	S&P 500	Expected Return*	Volatility*	Typical Range of Results**
1	100%	0%	7%	±0%	7%
2	67	33	9	±7	2% to 16
3	50	50	10	±10.5	−.5% to 20.5
4	33	67	11	±14	−3% to 25
5	0	100	13	±21	−8% to 34

*Calculated as the weighted average of the expected returns and volatilities of Treasury bills and the S&P 500. For example, for portfolio 2 above which is made up of 67% Treasury bills and 33% the S&P 500:

Portfolio expected return = .67(7%) + .33(13%) = 9%

Portfolio volatility = .67(0%) + .33(21%) = 7%

**There are two chances out of three that the actual return will be in a range defined by the expected return plus or minus the volatility.
Note: As the percentage allocated to the S&P 500 increases, the portfolio volatility increases much more rapidly than the incremental increase in expected return. The longer the time horizon, the more worthwhile it is to bear higher levels of short-run volatility. In deciding how they would divide their investment funds between Treasury bills and the S&P 500, clients are forced to acknowledge and deal with the risk/return trade-off issue.

because the alternative requires the rejection of more than six decades of historical relationships in favor of a different investment world view.[1]

By dividing the 21 percent standard deviation of common stocks by the 6 percent presumed equity risk premium, we see that for every 1 percent increase in the portfolio's expected return, portfolio volatility will increase by plus or minus 3.5 percent. For example, portfolio 2 has two thirds of its assets in Treasury bills, with one third in the S&P

---

[1]We will see later that on a portfolio basis using multiple asset categories, incremental returns are possible with less risk than this simple "two-investment alternative world" indicates. In working with clients, however, it is better to avoid holding out such hope at this point in the decision-making process.

500, and has an expected return of 9 percent. In order to increase the expected return by only 2 percent more, we need to shift an additional 33 percent of the portfolio out of Treasury bills into the S&P 500. Doing so, however, increases portfolio volatility by an additional plus or minus 7 percent! Awareness of this trade-off forces the client to focus more attention on his ability to tolerate the risk of short-run portfolio volatility. This process is healthy because in determining overall portfolio balance it is more important to concentrate on risk tolerance than on return requirement. Most clients require unusually high rates of return to achieve all of their goals. These high rates of return are often not realistically possible, given reasonable capital market expectations. Even if they are possible, they should not be pursued unless the client has the capacity to tolerate the associated risks. Having reviewed the historical performance of the capital markets, a client should have developed an awareness that the higher returns from equity investments are the compensation one expects to receive in exchange for the volatility assumed. A client's risk tolerance, in this framework, is simply the added volatility he is willing to accept in exchange for an extra unit of expected return. If the return associated with a client's maximum risk tolerance is insufficient to realize his goals, he should either modify his goals or acknowledge that they will most likely not be realized. If the return associated with the upper limit of his risk tolerance is more than is needed to accomplish his objectives, it is easy to move down to a more conservative portfolio.

Psychologically, it is easier to tolerate risk if the outcome occurs in the distant future. A proper understanding of time horizon, therefore, increases risk tolerance for the long time horizon investor. Unfortunately, however, the liquidity of the capital markets provides constant revision of security prices and a heightened awareness of short-run performance. The trick is to avoid attaching too much significance to short-run performance numbers if the relevant outcome is truly associated with a long-term time horizon.

Table 6–2 by itself may be sufficient for use by those clients who have a good intuitive grasp of the impact that the passage of time has on narrowing the range of portfolio compound returns. Other clients may need to have the range of returns over time for each portfolio specified in more detail. For them, Figures 6–1 through 6–5 can be used in conjunction with Table 6–2 to communicate the impact time has on the choice of portfolio balance. For those who like graphs, the distribution of returns for a 1-year time horizon is shown in Figures 6–2A through Figure 6–5A for portfolios 2 through 5. (Please note that in these graphs, different horizontal scales are used for each of the portfolios.) No such distribution is shown for portfolio 1 because it has a fixed annual return of 7 percent. Figures 6–2B through 6–5B show in tabular form the "distribution of portfolio annualized returns" which describe the likelihood of achieving various returns over 1-, 3-, 5-, 10-, 15-, and 25-year time horizons. Finally, Figures 6–1 and 6–2C through 6–5C show the path of wealth accumulation over time for each of the five portfolios for the tenth, fiftieth, and ninetieth percentile compound return probabilities.

(Text continues on p. 111.)

FIGURE 6–1
Portfolio 1

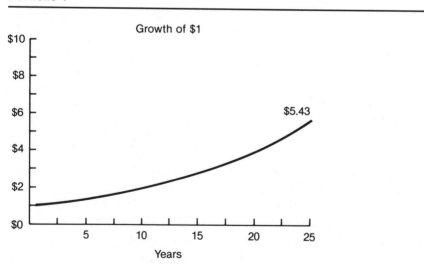

Growth of $1

Source: Illustration produced using Vestek Systems, Inc. software.

FIGURE 6-2
Portfolio 2

A. Distribution of returns; one-year time horizon

Annual rate of return

B. Distribution of portfolio annualized returns

Year	1st %	10th %	25th %	50th %	75th %	90th %	99th %
1	−6.30	0.19	4.17	8.78	13.58	18.10	26.28
3	−0.20	3.73	6.09	8.78	11.53	14.06	18.56
5	1.75	4.85	6.69	8.78	10.90	12.85	16.28
10	3.76	5.98	7.30	8.78	10.27	11.64	14.03
15	4.66	6.49	7.57	8.78	10.00	11.11	13.05
25	5.58	7.00	7.84	8.78	9.72	10.58	12.07

C. Growth of $1

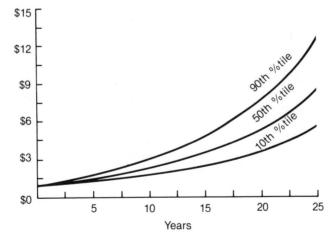

Years

Source: Illustrations produced using Vestek Systems, Inc. software.

FIGURE 6–3
Portfolio 3

A. Distribution of returns; one-year time horizon

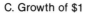

Annual rate of return

B. Distribution of portfolio annualized returns

Year	1st %	10th %	25th %	50th %	75th %	90th %	99th %
1	– 12.26	– 3.08	2.69	9.50	16.76	23.72	36.66
3	– 3.64	2.05	5.52	9.50	13.64	17.50	24.44
5	– 0.83	3.68	6.40	9.50	12.69	15.65	20.91
10	2.09	5.35	7.30	9.50	11.75	13.81	17.45
15	3.41	6.10	7.70	9.50	11.33	13.01	15.95
25	4.76	6.86	8.11	9.50	10.92	12.21	14.46

C. Growth of $1

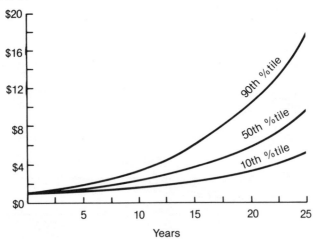

Years

Source: Illustrations produced using Vestek Systems, Inc. software.

FIGURE 6–4
Portfolio 4

A. Distribution of returns; one-year time horizon

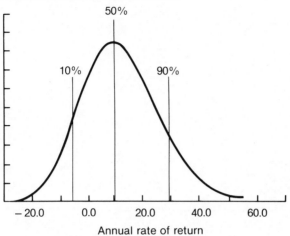

Annual rate of return

B. Distribution of portfolio annualized returns

Year	1st %	10th %	25th %	50th %	75th %	90th %	99th %
1	−17.78	−6.26	1.19	10.13	19.86	29.37	47.51
3	−6.97	0.35	4.87	10.13	15.65	20.86	30.37
5	−3.36	2.47	6.04	10.13	14.38	18.35	25.50
10	0.41	4.66	7.22	10.13	13.12	15.88	20.79
15	2.12	5.64	7.75	10.13	12.56	14.80	18.76
25	3.88	6.64	8.28	10.13	12.01	13.73	16.76

C. Growth of $1

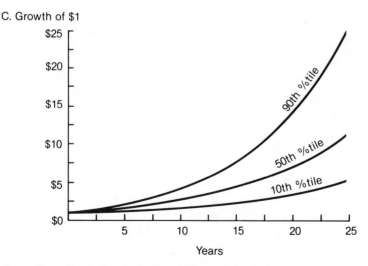

Years

Source: Illustrations produced using Vestek Systems, Inc. software.

109

FIGURE 6-5
Portfolio 5

A. Distribution of returns; one-year time horizon

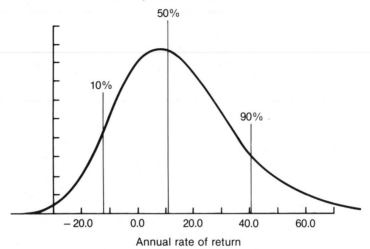

Annual rate of return

B. Distribution of portfolio annualized returns

Year	1st %	10th %	25th %	50th %	75th %	90th %	99th %
1	− 27.63	− 12.28	− 1.88	11.10	25.79	40.70	70.55
3	− 13.26	− 3.07	3.41	11.10	19.36	27.33	42.29
5	− 8.28	− 0.04	5.10	11.10	17.44	23.48	34.57
10	− 2.98	3.10	6.82	11.10	15.55	19.71	27.22
15	− 0.54	4.52	7.59	11.10	14.72	18.09	24.10
25	1.97	5.97	8.37	11.10	13.89	16.47	21.04

C. Growth of $1

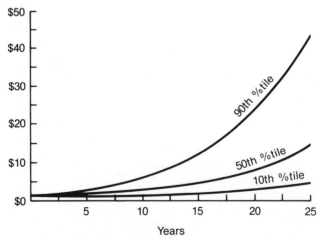

Years

Source: Illustrations produced using Vestek Systems, Inc. software.

As we review the distribution of portfolio annualized returns for portfolio 3 in Figure 6–3B, we see that −3.08 percent is shown at the tenth percentile for a 1-year time horizon. This means that there is a 90 percent likelihood that the actual return will be higher than −3.08 percent and a 10 percent likelihood that it will be lower. Under the tenth percentile column for a 5-year time horizon, however, we see a value of 3.68 percent. That is, there is a 90 percent likelihood that for a 5-year holding period, this portfolio will have a compound annual return in excess of 3.68 percent. For a 25-year horizon, there is a 90 percent likelihood that the compound annual return will be greater than 6.86 percent. As expected, with longer time horizons there are more opportunities for good and bad years to offset each other, thereby narrowing the range of outcomes. Under the twenty-fifth percentile column we find a value of 2.69 percent for a 1-year time horizon. That indicates that the chances are three out of four that the portfolio return will exceed 2.69 percent over a 1-year time horizon, and so forth.

If we compare portfolio 2 with portfolio 3 we will find that the expected return is lower and that the range of possible outcomes for any comparative time period is correspondingly less for portfolio 2. By contrast, portfolio 4 will have wider ranges of outcomes with a correspondingly higher expected return.[2]

A comparison of these exhibits shows the variation in short-run volatility based on the percentage of the portfolio allocated to the S&P 500. It also clearly demonstrates that the passage of time dramatically narrows the range of outcomes for each portfolio. This is consistent with the conclu-

---

[2]With a normal distribution, the range of returns is symmetrically distributed around the expected return. In reality, security returns are better described by a lognormal distribution which has a longer right tail. This is because it is impossible to lose more than 100 percent of your money, but the upside is open-ended. With a "right-tailed" lognormal distribution, the range is *not* symmetrically distributed around the expected return. The graphs and tables in Figures 6–2 through 6–5 utilize the more realistic lognormal distribution assumption.

sions reached in Chapter 5, which dealt with the importance of time horizon.

Investment objectives are usually solicited from clients during the initial data-gathering session. Occasionally a client will express an objective of "15 percent compound returns with little or no risk" which qualitatively translated would be "long-term growth of capital with stable principal values." This is not one investment objective, it is two competing objectives, and to the extent to which one objective is pursued the other must be sacrificed. This is simply the risk/return trade-off implicit among the choices in Table 6-2. We now have an appreciation of the necessity of educating your client and providing him with a context for making good decisions. According to Charles D. Ellis, portfolio balance decisions are investment policy decisions, which are the undelegatable responsibility of the *client*. Within the framework developed, the client's choice of portfolios from Table 6-2 is an indirect measure of the client's *informed* risk tolerance. This model is not without its drawbacks. The notion of "expected return" and "standard deviation" are not well understood by most clients. For this reason, the model has been designed to be as simple and straightforward as possible. There is also a risk of the choices being too hypothetical and therefore not realistic to clients. This can be overcome by incorporating discussions of historical capital market experiences like 1973-1974 when common stocks lost more than 40 percent of their value. Such market declines have occurred in the past, and will surely happen again in the future. Clients should be educated to expect that.

This exercise for determining broad portfolio balance should be engaged in periodically with clients. Over time, their experiences with investments will change and their reactions may differ from what was initially expected. For example, some clients who thought they thoroughly understood common stock volatility and could live with it may temper their opinions following an October 1987 stock market crash. Various life events can also occur, which alter risk tolerance. Examples are changes in family composition, job or career changes, or health problems. Through these changes this decision-making model will continue, however, to emphasize the fact that to increase expected return, one must willingly accept increased uncertainty. The balance chosen between interest-generating assets, as represented by Treasury bills, and equity investments, as represented by the S&P 500, is the most important investment decision the client will make. It determines simultaneously the risk and return characteristics of the portfolio. Subject to this basic policy decision, the adviser can proceed to design a more broadly diversified portfolio, utilizing multiple asset categories. This brings us to the next chapter, which deals with diversification.

CHAPTER 7

DIVERSIFICATION: THE THIRD DIMENSION

Better a steady dime than a rare dollar.

—Anonymous

Diversification in its naive sense is simply avoiding "putting all of your eggs in one basket." Certainly there is value in averaging out one's risks in a number of different investments, but diversification is both more powerful and more subtle than this. In this chapter we will explore the concept of diversification and find that our prior two-dimensional world, which describes an investment in terms of its risk and return, is inadequate. We need also to describe investments along a third dimension, which we will call the *diversification effect.*

Figure 7-1 shows two investments, A and B, each of which have similar risk/return characteristics. They also move in lockstep with one another. As investment A moves up, so does investment B. As investment A loses value, so does investment B. A statistician would describe this relationship as one of "perfect positive cross-correlation." If we invest half our money in investment A and half in investment B, we will have a portfolio result that follows the path of the dotted line in Figure 7-1. The return on this portfolio will simply be a weighted average of the returns of the two investments that constitute the portfolio. Similarly, *because they move in lockstep with one another,* the risk of the portfolio will be a weighted average of the risks of the two investments. In this example we have only an averaging

FIGURE 7-1

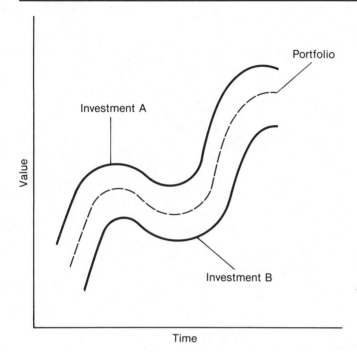

of risks—our eggs are in two baskets rather than one. As
we will define the term, there is no diversification effect, as
these assets are combined to form a portfolio.

In Figure 7-2 we again have two investments, C and D.
As in Figure 7-1, they have the same return characteristics.
They also have the same risk as measured by their respective volatilities. But unlike the situation in Figure 7-1, investments C and D move in opposite cycles. As investment C
gains value, investment D loses value and vice versa. This is
an example of "perfect negative cross-correlation." With half
our money allocated to investment C and half allocated to
investment D, this countercyclical pattern of returns produces a marvelous portfolio result, as indicated by the dotted
line in Figure 7-2. The return on the portfolio is again simply a weighted average of the returns of the two investments
that compose the portfolio. But, rather than simply averag-

FIGURE 7-2

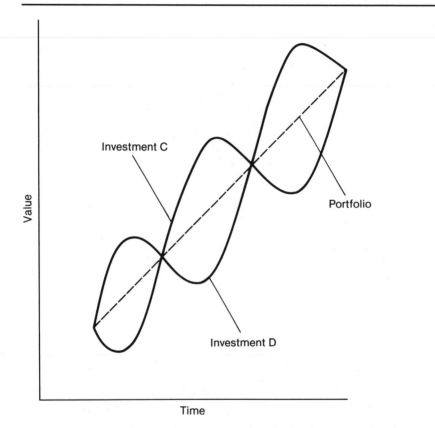

Time

ing our risks as we did in Figure 7-1, we have completely eliminated the risk of the portfolio in Figure 7-2. Diversification effect is at a maximum in the situation illustrated in Figure 7-2, as these assets combine to build a portfolio. Such perfectly negatively correlated investments generally do not exist in the real world. If they did, no investors would buy risk-free Treasury bills yielding 7 percent when they could buy two risky assets and combine them in such a manner as to produce a riskless 9 percent.

In Figure 7-3, we have two more investments, E and F, with similar risk (volatility) and return characteristics. This is the middle ground situation where the investments

FIGURE 7-3

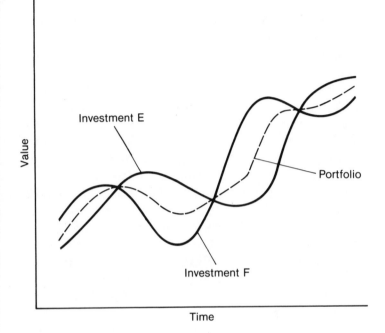

are neither perfectly positively nor perfectly negatively correlated. We can see periods of time when the investments tend to move together and the diversification effect is weak, and other times when they move in different directions, with stronger diversification effect on the portfolio. This is more representative of "real world" investment situations. As in the other two examples, the portfolio return is a weighted average of the returns of the investments that compose the portfolio. But, the diversification effect associated with the dissimilar patterns of return has partially eliminated the risk on a portfolio basis.

Statisticians use the measurement called *cross-correlation* (or simply correlation) *of returns* between two investments to indicate the extent to which knowledge of one return provides information regarding the behavior of the other. For example, the perfect positive correlation, such as found between investments A and B in Figure 7–1, is described by a correlation of +1.0. The perfect negative correlation between investments C and D in Figure 7–2 is described by a correlation of −1.0. All correlation measures are bound by these two extremes. Patterns of return that are unrelated to one another (i.e., neither positive nor negative correlation) have correlations near 0.[1]

In each of the examples we gave, the portfolio return is simply a weighted average of the returns of the investments that compose the portfolio. This will always be the case, regardless of the pattern of returns among the investments. The portfolio risk, however, will be *less* than the weighted average of the risk levels of the assets in the portfolio in all cases except the rare situation of perfect positive correlation among investments. This is due to the diversification effect of investments whose patterns of return partially offset one another, thereby somewhat smoothing portfolio volatility. Diversification is much more than simply not putting all your eggs in one basket. We can also see clearly why measures of the risk and return characteristics of individual investments are inadequate in describing what happens when investments are combined in forming portfolios. Diversification effect, as measured by the correlation of returns among investment alternatives, provides the third measurement dimension needed.

How do these concepts apply in the real world? Let us turn our discussion to bonds and common stocks, which are the primary blocks of traditional investment portfolios. In Chapter 2 we learned that from 1926 through 1988 common stocks had a compound annual return of 10.0 percent with a standard deviation of 20.9 percent, whereas long-term cor-

---

[1]The *covariance* of two investments' returns is a weighted average of the products of the deviations of the returns around their expected returns, where the probabilities of the deviations are used as weights. The *cross-correlation* of two investments' returns is equal to their covariance divided by the product of their standard deviations.

porate bonds had a compound annual return of 5.0 percent with a standard deviation of 8.4 percent.[2] The correlation between bond and stock returns over this same period was +.19. If we assume that the future will be like the past (a big assumption, as we will see) then the range of portfolio possibilities using common stocks and corporate bonds is described in Figure 7-4. Point B represents an all-bond portfolio and point S represents an all-stock portfolio. Notice how the curved line of portfolio possibilities represents a substantial improvement over the straight dashed line connecting point B and point S. This diversification effect is driven by the low stock/bond correlation of +.19.

The risk/return characteristics of, and correlation between, stocks and bonds as described in the preceding paragraph are based on the entire 63-year period 1926 through 1988. It is important to keep in mind, however, that there has been, and will continue to be, considerable variability in these relative performance numbers. For example, Figure 7-5 compares the five-year compound annual returns of common stocks versus long-term corporate bonds on a rolling monthly basis. The dominance of common stock returns over corporate bonds is very apparent. But we can also see that over periods as short as five years, the higher volatility associated with common stocks will result in many instances when their returns will lag that available from bonds. This highlights the danger of putting too much attention on the long-term relationships among expected returns for various investment alternatives, without simultaneously considering the uncertainty in those relationships. This is true particularly in the short-run, where high standard devi-

---

[2]It should be noted that the standard deviations are actually around the arithmetic means rather than the geometric means (compound annual returns). Because we have built our models within the context of average compound return relationships over multiple-time periods, I will continue to use compound annual return numbers even though in a single-period context it would be more appropriate to use arithmetic means.

FIGURE 7–4
Corporate Bond/Common Stock

Portfolio possibilities

Source: Illustration produced using Vestek Systems, Inc. software.

ations can produce short-term and intermediate-term experiences that differ considerably from long-term experience. It is therefore important for advisers to guide their clients through the exercise of developing models of long-term relationships among investment alternatives, while simultaneously emphasizing that short-term experiences will widely vary.

Figure 7–6 graphs on a rolling monthly basis, the five-year standard deviations of returns for common stocks

FIGURE 7-5
Common Stocks versus Corporate Bonds. Compound Annual Returns (1926–1988)

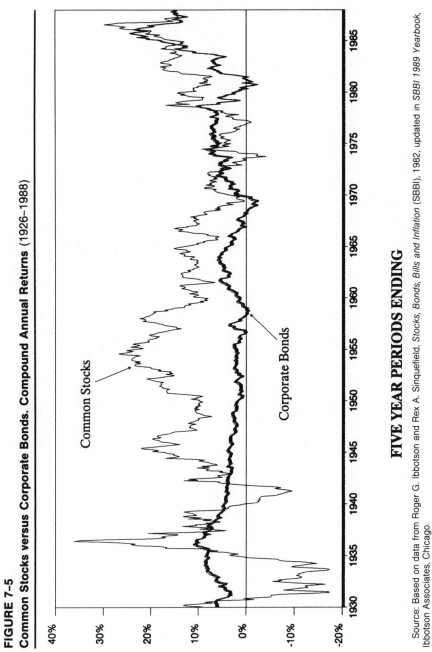

FIVE YEAR PERIODS ENDING

Source: Based on data from Roger G. Ibbotson and Rex A. Sinquefield, *Stocks, Bonds, Bills and Inflation* (SBBI), 1982, updated in *SBBI 1989 Yearbook*, Ibbotson Associates, Chicago.

FIGURE 7-6
Common Stocks versus Corporate Bonds. Standard Deviations of Returns (1926–1988)

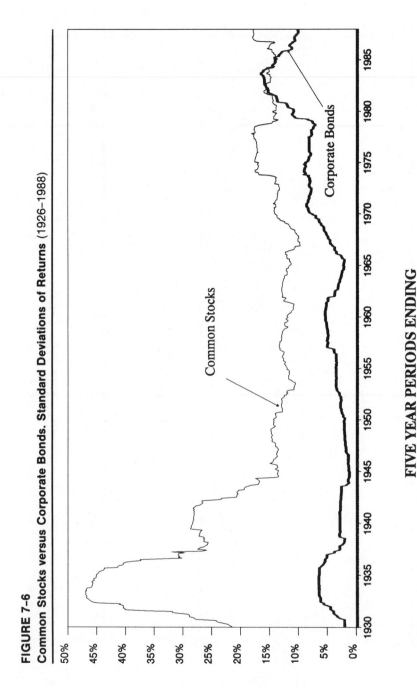

FIVE YEAR PERIODS ENDING

Source: Based on data from Roger G. Ibbotson and Rex A. Sinquefield, *Stocks, Bonds, Bills and Inflation* (SBBI), 1982, updated in *SBBI 1989 Yearbook*, Ibbotson Associates, Chicago.

versus long-term corporate bonds. Table 3–1 from Chapter 3 indicated that, based on the entire period 1926 through 1988, the standard deviation of returns was 20.9 percent for common stocks and 8.4 percent for corporate bonds. We can see, however, from Figure 7–6 that the volatility of both stocks and bonds has varied widely over time. Common stocks had their highest volatility during the period preceding World War II. Bonds on the other hand, had low volatility until the mid-1960s when volatility began to increase dramatically through the 1980s as a result of a rapidly changing interest rate environment.

The five-year correlation between common stock and corporate bond returns is graphed on a rolling monthly basis in Figure 7–7. For this entire 63-year period, the correlation was +.19. But we can see that it has actually varied widely from a high of +.62 to a low of −.28. It is during the periods of negative correlation that the strongest diversification effect will be produced, offering investors great advantages in risk reduction for having both represented in a portfolio.

In the next chapter, we will discuss the mathematics of portfolio optimization, which identifies "ideal asset mixes" *based on the inputs* to a computer program. The output from such programs is highly sensitive to the inputs. One purpose in reviewing Figures 7–5 through 7–7 is to increase one's awareness of the uncertainty inherent in the inputs upon which these computer programs rely. At best, historical data is *helpful* in understanding investment asset risk/return characteristics and relationships. It cannot, however, be massaged in such a way to extract "the truth" from what is basically an uncertain process.

When we examine the range of portfolio possibilities utilizing only two investment alternatives, each level of portfolio expected return has a unique asset allocation associated with it. This is not true when we consider the range of portfolio possibilities when utilizing three or more investment alternatives. A wide range of asset allocations may be identified, all of which produce the same portfolio expected return but with different levels of risk. Obviously, the optimal asset allocation for a particular portfolio expected return is

FIGURE 7-7

Common Stocks versus Corporate Bonds. Cross-Correlation of Returns (1926–1988)

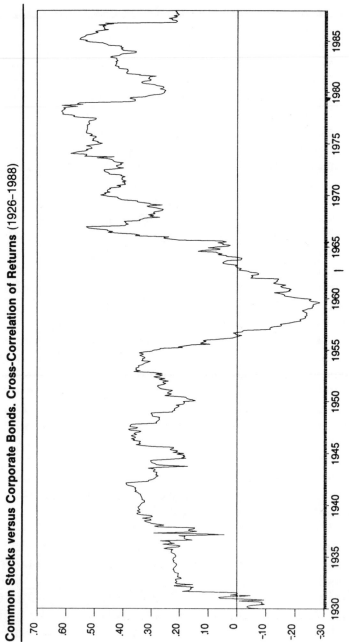

FIVE YEAR PERIODS ENDING

Source: Based on data from Roger G. Ibbotson and Rex A. Sinquefield, *Stocks, Bonds, Bills and Inflation* (SBBI), 1982, updated in *SBBI 1989 Yearbook*, Ibbotson Associates, Chicago.

that unique allocation which minimizes portfolio risk. Other asset allocations are undesirable because of their unnecessarily high levels of risk. By definition, a portfolio that minimizes portfolio risk for a given expected return (or equivalently maximizes portfolio expected return for a given level of risk) is said to be *efficient*. If we join together all the efficient portfolios for a given set of investment alternatives, we form what is called the *efficient frontier*.

We intuitively understand the wisdom of not putting all of our eggs in one basket, and we know that it is important to understand the risk/return characteristics of each basket we use. Earlier in this chapter we gained an appreciation of the importance of also considering how the various baskets behave relative to one another in reducing risk on a portfolio basis through the diversification effect. Now we have gone an additional step in emphasizing that it is also important to determine the *right amount* to place in each of the baskets in order to have an efficient portfolio.

The implications of this last realization are important. There are good and bad allocations of assets within any portfolio, and the objective is to allocate assets in such a way as to own a portfolio that lies on the efficient frontier. These portfolios have less risk than any other portfolio with equivalent expected return, or alternatively, have more return than any other portfolio with equivalent risk.

Inefficient portfolios should be avoided because they incur unnecessary risks that could be eliminated with proper rebalancing. Sometimes, the idea of an inefficient portfolio sounds like evidence against the notion of the risk/return trade-off we worked so hard to establish and describe earlier in Chapter 6. Before, we were told that the only way to increase expected return was to increase risk. Now we are told that we can improve the return on an inefficient portfolio without increasing risk. Isn't this a contradiction? No. The risk/return trade-off is alive and well, living on the efficient frontier! That is, presuming that you now have an efficient portfolio, the only way to increase the expected return (if constrained to a given set of investment alternatives) is to increase portfolio risk.

Another possible reaction to the notion of inefficient portfolios is the apparent existence of an economic "free lunch." Here is a situation where it is possible to pick up incremental return for free. Yet, in an efficient market there are no free lunches. Rather than this situation being thought of as a "free lunch," an inefficient portfolio can be more appropriately considered to be a situation where risk is needlessly incurred without compensation, or where alternatively, incremental returns are unnecessarily sacrificed.

If we extend our diversification example by adding a fourth investment alternative with different risk/return characteristics than the other three, we now have even more options to consider in building our portfolios. The new investment alternative provides the *possibility* of further portfolio risk reduction at various levels of expected return. (The word *possibility* is italicized because the addition of a new investment alternative does not guarantee the advisability of its utilization.) If the risk/return characteristics of this fourth investment alternative provide less risky ways of building portfolios for various levels of expected return, then a new efficient frontier will be formed above the old one, as shown in Figure 7-8.

By expanding the menu of investment alternatives to be used as possible building blocks for the portfolio, there exist more opportunities to earn increasingly higher returns at whatever level of risk one can tolerate. Alternatively, we can view the increasing number of alternatives as providing more opportunities to reduce risk at whatever level of expected return one seeks. The message is clear: Although it is not always advisable to utilize all the investment alternatives provided in a given situation, it is always preferable to have more, rather than fewer, investment alternatives from which to choose. Any time investment alternatives are artificially restricted, the risk is incurred that the investor will be confined to a choice along a lower efficient frontier than would otherwise be possible.

Although the diversification effect is usually thought of in terms of risk reduction, it equivalently can be viewed in terms of return enhancement. This is important because ag-

FIGURE 7-8
Three versus Four Investment Alternative Efficient Frontiers

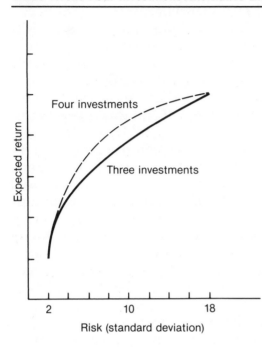

gressive investors are often not interested in discussing diversification strategies because they believe that diversification will impair returns. Not so! In essence, diversification effect enables the more aggressive investor to improve returns through the commitment of an even greater percentage of his portfolio to equity investments than would otherwise be possible without the smoothing effect of partially offsetting patterns of returns.

If we wanted to eliminate as much risk as possible from our portfolio, we might consider taking diversification to its logical conclusion by representing all major investment alternatives in our portfolio. This would provide the greatest opportunity for dissimilar patterns of return among investments to partially offset one another. Would this, however, eliminate all portfolio risk? No. The remaining risk exists despite diversification, and so we will call it *nondiversifiable risk.* When we think about bearing unavoidable risks, we expect to be commensurately rewarded. For example, in Chapter 6 we devised a hypothetical world composed of only two investment alternatives—Treasury bills and the S&P 500. In this world, the only route to an improved expected return was through the assumption of the risk of the S&P 500. So we expect to be rewarded for bearing unavoidable risks.

But what about the kind of risk that can be easily eliminated through diversification? We will call this *diversifiable risk.* Should we be rewarded for bearing it? By analogy, consider a fireman who deserves to be well-compensated because of the risks inherent in his occupation. One day he heroically enters a burning building to successfully save a child from the flames. For this and other similar acts of courage and skill he receives a promotion with a pay raise. During a subsequent fire he hears the screams of another young child, but before entering the burning building he takes off his asbestos suit and, wearing only his underwear, rescues the child. The next day he approaches the firechief and asks for a raise because of the increased risks he took in rescuing the child. What will be the firechief's response?

One big lesson of modern portfolio theory is that in an efficient market, there is no compensation for bearing risks that can be easily avoided. Diversifiable risk therefore deserves and receives no compensation. For example, Figure 7-9 describes the risk characteristics of two stocks, A and B. Initially, one might naively conclude that stock A, with its greater total risk, will be priced to provide for a greater expected return than that of stock B. But we can see that in this example, stock B has more nondiversifiable risk than stock A and, accordingly, will be priced by the marketplace to produce a higher expected return than stock A!

One very practical implication of this discussion is the risk unnecessarily assumed by anyone who commits a disproportionately large share of his portfolio to one investment position. Consider a client who has 90 percent of his investment portfolio allocated to the stock of one large publicly traded corporation. He obviously has retained much diversifiable risk *which is not priced by the marketplace to*

FIGURE 7-9

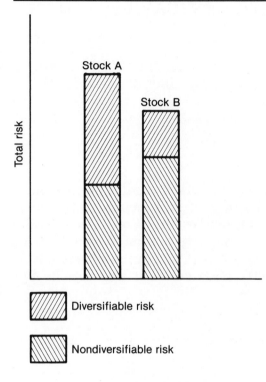

reward *him or anyone else.* This is the situation of the fireman who takes off his asbestos suit to run into a burning building to save a child from the flames. The pricing mechanism of an efficient market in effect assumes that investors are smart enough to eliminate diversifiable risk through broad diversification. Those who do not diversify pay the price of assuming unnecessary risks. The argument for diversifying a client's portfolio away from overconcentration in one stock obviously goes beyond the notion of simply not putting all of your eggs in one basket.

The Appendix that follows is written for readers who are interested in a more detailed discussion of the concepts developed in this chapter. Those who are not interested in further elaboration can safely proceed to the next chapter.

APPENDIX: A MORE DETAILED DISCUSSION OF DIVERSIFICATION CONCEPTS

Consider two investments, X and Y, with expected returns and risks as measured by their standard deviations of:

Investment	Expected Return	Risk
X	10%	18%
Y	8%	10%

Figure 7-10 shows these two investments plotted in a risk/return space. Initially one might presume that investment portfolios built using those two investments would plot along the straight line connecting points X and Y. This would be true, however, only if the correlation of returns between X and Y is perfectly positive, as it was for the two

FIGURE 7-10

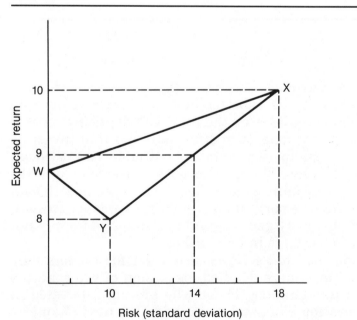

investments in Figure 7-1. To get an expected return of 9 percent for example, one would have to be willing to accept a risk level of 14 percent. (This can be seen by noting the distance on the horizontal axis corresponding to the point where a horizontal line drawn from an expected return of 9 percent intercepts the straight line connecting points X and Y.)

The opposite extreme is where X and Y are perfectly negatively correlated in a fashion similar to the two investments in Figure 7-2. Let us start at point Y with 100 percent of the portfolio committed to investment Y. As we begin to reallocate some money to investment X, we begin moving the portfolio along the line connecting point Y to point W. At point W, we have almost two thirds of our money in investment Y, with the remainder in investment X. With this asset allocation, the perfect countercyclical pattern of returns has completely eliminated risk on a portfolio level—portfolio W has an expected return of 8.7 percent with no risk! As we further increase the percentage of the portfolio allocated to investment X, the portfolio moves along the line connecting point W to point X until the point is reached where 100 percent of the portfolio is committed to investment X.

The curved line of Figure 7-11 connecting point Y with point X describes the more typical situation of neither perfectly positive nor perfectly negative correlation. Assume, for example, that we want to achieve a 9 percent expected return from a portfolio composed of investments X and Y. A horizontal line drawn from the 9 percent point on the vertical axis intercepts the curved line at a point corresponding to a risk level of 11 percent. Note that this horizontal line would intercept a straight line connecting point Y and point X at a risk level of 14 percent. In essence, the difference between this 14 percent risk level (which assumes perfect positive correlation and hence, no diversification effect) and the 11 percent risk level implied by the curved line represents the reduction in portfolio risk associated with the diversification effect.

Although the diversification effect is usually thought of in terms of risk reduction, it can equivalently be viewed

FIGURE 7-11

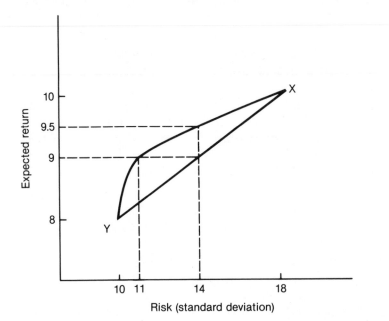

Risk (standard deviation)

in terms of return enhancement. Returning to Figure 7-11, for example, if we are willing to live with a risk level of 14 percent, we would have to accept an expected return of 9 percent if X and Y were perfectly positively correlated. Because they are not, we can obtain an expected return of 9.5 percent. This is the vertical height corresponding to a point where a vertical line drawn from a risk level of 14 percent intercepts the curved line. This extra .5 percent in expected return is equivalently attributable to diversification effect.

Thus far, we have discussed diversification in the context of two investment alternatives. In this situation, each unique combination of the two investments is associated with a particular expected return. For example, in Figure 7-11, an expected return of 9 percent is associated with only one specific combination of investments X and Y. Lowering the percentage allocated to X produces a lower expected return for the portfolio, while increasing the percentage allocated to X increases the expected return. Let us now consider diversification in a situation involving multiple investment alternatives, X, Y, and Z, with the following risk/return characteristics:

Investment	Expected Return	Standard Deviation
X	10%	18%
Y	8%	10%
Z	6%	2%

With three investment alternatives, we need to specify three correlations. This is usually done in the form of a correlation matrix:

	X	Y	Z
X	1.00		
Y	.50	1.00	
Z	.10	.30	1.00

With three or more investment alternatives, we no longer have unique solutions associated with various expected returns. For example, we can build any number of different investment portfolios to obtain an expected return of 8 percent. Some examples are:

Portfolio	Percentage Allocation to Investment			Portfolio Expected Return	Portfolio Standard Deviation
	X	Y	Z		
1	0	100	0	8	10.0
2	50	0	50	8	9.2
3	30	40	30	8	8.3
4	25	50	25	8	8.4

Of the four choices listed, portfolio 3 is the best because it produces the expected return of 8 percent with the least risk, as measured by the portfolio standard deviation. But, can this portfolio be improved? Is there some other asset allocation that can produce the same expected return of 8 percent with even less portfolio risk? Although there are an infinite number of different portfolio allocations that can produce the desired expected return of 8 percent, there is only one specific allocation that will push portfolio risk to its minimum possible value. The same is true for any specific return between the maximum return of 10 percent associated with investment X and the return associated with the lowest risk portfolio composed of investments X, Y, and Z. Due to the diversification effect, it is possible that this lowest risk portfolio may have a higher expected return *with less risk* than investment Z! With respect to *any* specific expected return within that range, there are an infinite number of portfolio allocations that can produce a specified expected return, but there is only one unique allocation that optimally produces the specific expected return with a minimum of portfolio risk.

The specific allocation that minimizes portfolio risk for a given expected return is considered *optimal*. By definition, these optimal portfolios are said to be *efficient*. Other portfolios that produce the same expected return, but with greater risk, are said to be *inefficient*. If we connect each of the optimal portfolios associated with each possible level of expected return, we would form what is called the *efficient frontier*.

Let us now approach the subject of diversification from yet another direction. Assume we have a large collection of risky assets. Figure 7-12 shows each asset plotted in terms of its risk/return characteristics. As we consider the nature of the risk/return trade-off, we would perhaps expect to see these assets form a pattern that slopes upward to the right. Yet we see no such pattern. The reason for this will become clear later.

Now consider the portfolio possibilities based on various combinations and weightings of these risky assets. Figure 7-13 shows this set of possible portfolios as the shaded area bound on the upper left by the efficient frontier connecting points A and B. Obviously, we again see that for any given expected return, there are good (efficient) and bad (inefficient) ways to combine assets to build portfolios. If we are limited to choosing from only these risky assets in building our portfolios, we should choose a portfolio lying somewhere along the curved efficient frontier connecting point A with point B.

FIGURE 7-12

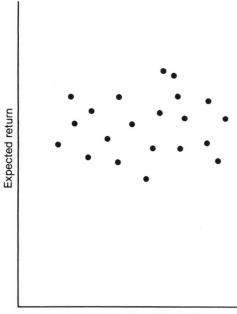

Risk (standard deviation)

What would happen if we change the example by permitting investors to either borrow money or invest it at some risk-free rate of interest "R_f?" Figure 7-14 shows a line drawn from point C corresponding to R_f on the vertical axis to the point of tangency M on the efficient frontier. In this situation, it is advantageous for *all* investors to hold the same optimal risky portfolio M, in combination with either borrowing or investing at the risk-free rate of interest in accordance with their risk tolerance.

Investors who are more risk-averse would invest part of their money at the risk-free rate of interest and hold the balance in the risky portfolio M. Depending on the percentage invested at the risk-free rate of interest, their portfolio would lie somewhere on the straight line connecting point C, corresponding to the risk-free rate of interest, and point M, the optimal risky portfolio. Investors with greater risk tolerance could hold investment portfolios lying along line MX by bor-

FIGURE 7-13

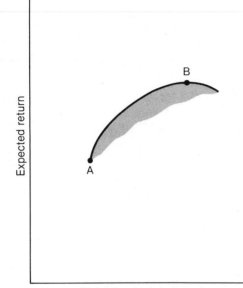

Risk (standard deviation)

rowing money at the risk-free rate of interest in order to provide additional funds for making larger investments in the optimal risky portfolio M. Note that with the added possibility of borrowing or lending, the portfolio possibilities on line CMX lie above, and are therefore superior to, those lying on the efficient frontier between points A and B, where borrowing or lending is not possible.

This leads to a discussion of the Capital Asset Pricing Model (CAPM) which was developed in the mid-1960s by William F. Sharpe in conjunction with other researchers. It provides a powerful description of the relationship between risk and return in an efficient capital market. As is the case with most models, simplifying assumptions are made to abstract the essence of the relationship being modeled. With the CAPM several such assumptions are made:

1. All investors are assumed to have the same investment information and to hold identical expectations regarding the future.

FIGURE 7-14

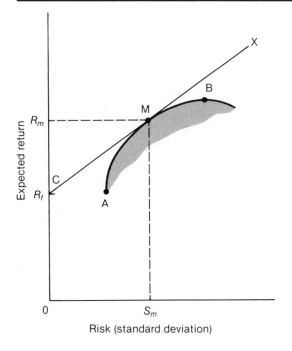

Risk (standard deviation)

2. The market is perfectly competitive.
3. There are no transaction costs for buying and selling securities.
4. Investors live in a tax-free world.
5. Investors can either invest or borrow at the same risk-free rate of interest.
6. Investors are risk-averse.

In such a world, all investors would create and hold the same efficient portfolio of risky assets. This is called the *market portfolio* and is composed of all risky investment assets, each weighted in terms of its outstanding market value. In order to accommodate for individual differences in risk tolerance, investors can either borrow or invest at the risk-free rate of interest in combination with holding the market portfolio. Let us now define point M in Figure 7-14 to be the market portfolio. The risk associated with the market portfolio is the nondiversifiable risk inherent in the market as a whole. This risk is quantified by the distance $0S_m$ on the horizontal axis. The expected return on the market is labeled on the vertical axis at R_m. Line CMX is known as the *capital market line*. It reflects the upward-sloping relationship between risk and return among the efficient investment strategies that lie on this line. The slope of the capital market line can be thought of as the reward one expects to receive per unit of risk borne.

Each risky asset in the market portfolio can have its total risk (standard deviation) broken down into diversifiable and nondiversifiable components. One powerful conclusion of the CAPM is that only the latter nondiversifiable component of total risk justifies extra compensation. Beta, β, is the measure of a risky asset's nondiversifiable risk relative to the market portfolio. It is computed by a statistical comparison of the asset's pattern of return relative to the return of the market portfolio.

We can now explain why the risky assets in Figure 7-12 do not form a pattern that slopes upward to the right. If diversifiable risk is not rewarded by the marketplace, then we should plot expected return against nondiversifiable risk (i.e., β) rather than against total risk as we did in Figure 7-12. A plot of this new relationship forms what is called the *Security Market Line* (SML) as shown in Figure 7-15. The SML begins at R_f and passes through point M which corresponds to the market portfolio. In equilibrium, the buying and selling activities of investors in an efficient capital market will price securities such that they fall on the SML. In other words, according to the CAPM, a security's expected return is a function of the risk-free rate of interest, the expected return on the market, and its nondiversifiable risk as measured by β. This is mathematically expressed by:

$R_i = R_f + (R_m - R_f)\ \beta_i$ where
R_i = expected return on security I
R_f = Risk-free rate of interest
R_m = Expected return on the market portfolio
β_i = Beta value for security I

FIGURE 7-15

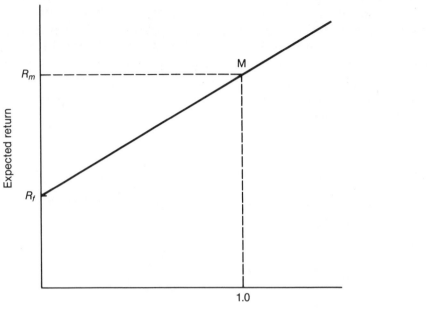

Most often, a broad-based stock index such as the S&P 500 is used as a proxy for the market portfolio. In this context, β is a measure of how an individual stock's return covaries with the S&P 500. Arguably, however, the S&P 500 is much too narrow a proxy for the market portfolio. By definition, the market portfolio should contain all investment assets, each weighted in terms of its outstanding market value. Hence, it would be more appropriate to describe the market portfolio in global terms, including both domestic and international stocks and bonds, real estate, and all other major investment asset categories. Such a market portfolio would look like Figure 1-1. In this context, β would be a measurement of each investment's pattern of return relative to this world market portfolio. By implication, all investors should hold the same world market portfolio, and adjust for risk-tolerance differences through either investing or borrowing at the risk-free rate of interest.

Various extended models of the original CAPM have been developed since the mid-1960s, as well as other models concerning security pricing.[3] The CAPM has been criticized on the basis of its unrealistic assumptions, and as not providing a completely accurate description of real-world security pricing. It nevertheless remains an extremely powerful model, highlighting the nature of the important risk/return relationship implicit in the way securities are priced in the marketplace.

---

[3]For example, Arbitrage Pricing Theory asserts that multiple factors, in addition to market risk, are involved in security pricing. For further discussion, the reader is directed to the academic literature on this subject.

CHAPTER 8

TRADITIONAL PORTFOLIOS VERSUS MORE BROADLY DIVERSIFIED APPROACHES

You pays your money and you takes your choice.
—Punch, 1846

Fifteen years ago, United States stocks and bonds constituted the majority of the world's total equity and debt markets. Our capital markets were not only the largest, they were also the most liquid and efficient. Our economy was broadly diversified, dynamic, and resilient. It is not surprising, therefore, that U.S. investors have traditionally held portfolios composed predominantly of domestic stocks and bonds. As a proxy for the "Traditional Portfolio" let us construct a portfolio that maintains an allocation of 10 percent Treasury bills, 40 percent long-term corporate bonds, and 50 percent S&P 500. By examining the Traditional Portfolio's investment performance for the period beginning in 1973 and ending with 1988, we will encompass bull and bear market conditions for both stocks and bonds. The 16-year compound return for this portfolio was 9.9 percent: the weighted average of the returns available from Treasury bills, long-term corporate bonds, and the S&P 500. The portfolio's standard deviation was 12.4 percent. Had more investment alternatives been utilized, however, the risk/return characteristics of the portfolio could have been improved.

In the past, the Traditional Portfolio was considered by many to be a good example of proper diversification. Today, its inadequacies are increasingly apparent. Figure 1-1 shows the estimated allocation of the world's total investable capital as of the end of 1988. By adding the percentage allocations for cash equivalents, U.S. bonds, and U.S. equities, we see that the Traditional Portfolio now represents only 40 percent of the world market capitalization.

Imagine for a moment that we have two competing investment organizations, alike in every way, except that one firm can invest internationally whereas the other is restricted to U.S. stocks and bonds. Each firm is well-staffed by highly qualified talented professionals with ready access to quality research services. Which firm is likely to deliver the better risk-adjusted performance results? All other things being equal, the international firm with its broader set of investment possibilities has a greater chance for better performance. The worse case for the international money management firm is that they will find no attractive investment opportunities outside of the United States. In this unlikely situation, they still have a 50/50 chance of outperforming the money management firm that is restricted to U.S. stocks and bonds. If, however, they find attractive investment opportunities not available to the domestic money management firm, the expectation is that their performance will be superior.

The other major investment alternatives represented in Figure 1-1 are international bonds, international stocks, and real estate. These investment alternatives, in addition to small company domestic stocks, provide an opportunity to greatly broaden the diversification of the Traditional Portfolio. The next several sections will provide an overview of each of these important investment alternatives.

SMALL COMPANY STOCKS

Even though a client may intellectually understand the advantages of a more broadly diversified strategy, the consideration of new investment alternatives often produces anxiety. The old and familiar is more comfortable than the new and different. For an investor who holds our hypothetical Traditional Portfolio of 10 percent Treasury bills, 40 percent long-term corporate bonds, and 50 percent S&P 500, the least-threatening diversification alternative will probably be small company stocks. An investor with a substantial commitment to the S&P 500 understands the potential risks and rewards of equity investing. By reviewing the historical performance of small stocks as we did in Chapter 2, the client will learn that historically small stocks have provided the highest returns of all of the domestic marketable investment alternatives reviewed by Ibbotson Associates. They have also had the highest risk as measured by the standard deviation of returns. Figure 8-1 compares the performance characteristics of small stocks versus the Traditional Portfolio for the past 16 years. The top graph compares the 3-year compound annual returns for each on a rolling monthly basis.[1] For most of this 16-year time period, small stocks had substantially higher returns than the Traditional Portfolio. Small stocks were likewise usually outperforming large capitalization stocks. The addition of small stocks to the Traditional Portfolio would therefore have generally boosted returns. But from mid-1983 through the end of 1987, small stock performance lagged that of large capitalization companies. (As we discussed in Chapter 3, there is a tendency for the small stock premium to follow a trend. Hence there may be prolonged periods of time when large capitalization stocks will outperform small stocks and vice versa.)

The middle graph in Figure 8-1 compares on a rolling monthly basis the three year standard deviations for each series of returns. As expected, small stock returns have been highly volatile and would have resulted in an increase in portfolio risk if utilized. The bottom graph shows the rolling three-year cross-correlation of returns for small stocks versus the Traditional Portfolio. It ranged from a low of .59 to

---

[1]For example, the first set of data points compares compound annual returns for the time period January 1973 through December 1975; the next set of data points compares compound annual returns for the time period February 1973 through January 1976, and so on.

COMPOUND ANNUAL RETURNS

THREE YEAR PERIODS ENDING

STANDARD DEVIATIONS OF RETURNS

THREE YEAR PERIODS ENDING

CROSS-CORRELATION OF RETURNS

THREE YEAR PERIODS ENDING

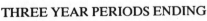

Source: Based on data from Roger G. Ibbotson and Rex A. Sinquefield, *Stocks, Bonds, Bills and Inflation* (SBBI), 1982, updated in *SBBI 1989 Yearbook*, Ibbotson Associates, Chicago.

a high of .88. Although this less than perfect cross-correlation would have produced some portfolio diversification effect, the much higher volatility of small stocks would have had a more powerful impact on the risk characteristics of the portfolio.

INTERNATIONAL STOCKS

International stock investing has increased substantially in the wake of wider acceptance over the past several years. This has been triggered by a variety of factors. First, the United States accounts for a shrinking percentage of world Gross National Product and world market capitalization. Second, many of the world's major corporations are non-U.S. and offer significant opportunities in certain market sectors. For example, Canada, South Africa, and Australia have major natural resource companies and West Germany, Japan, and Sweden all have major automobile manufacturing corporations. Many other countries have higher rates of savings, capital formation, and economic growth. The work ethic is also stronger in some countries, particularly in the Pacific Basin. Finally, many foreign stock markets have outperformed the U.S. stock market, and the relatively low cross-correlation of returns between the United States and foreign markets provides for substantial diversification effect in moderating portfolio risk. Figure 8–2, demonstrates the substantial historical improvement in a portfolio's risk/return characteristics which even modest international diversification can produce. For example, with each 10-year period examined, portfolio risk was significantly reduced with a 10 to 30 percent commitment to EAFE (Europe, Australia, Far East) securities. At the same time, portfolio return was either maintained or enhanced.

Figure 8–3 shows comparative performance statistics for international stocks versus the Traditional Portfolio. The international stock index used in these graphs was provided by Morgan Stanley Capital International Perspective. It measures the total return from a broad representation of

FIGURE 8-2
Long-Term: Increased Return and Reduced Risk

Source: Russell Analytical Services.

international common stocks from 20 foreign countries. International stocks on average had higher returns than the Traditional Portfolio, but with a higher standard deviation. The cross-correlation varied from a low of .12 to a high of .70. In general, the inclusion of international stocks would have significantly improved the risk/return characteristics of less well-diversified portfolios.

International investing is not without its special problems, however. Accounting practices in foreign countries differ from our own and often provide less complete disclosure to investors. Many foreign markets are not as liquid, nor are they as well-regulated as the U.S. stock market. This often

FIGURE 8-3
International Stocks versus the Traditional Portfolio (1973–1988)

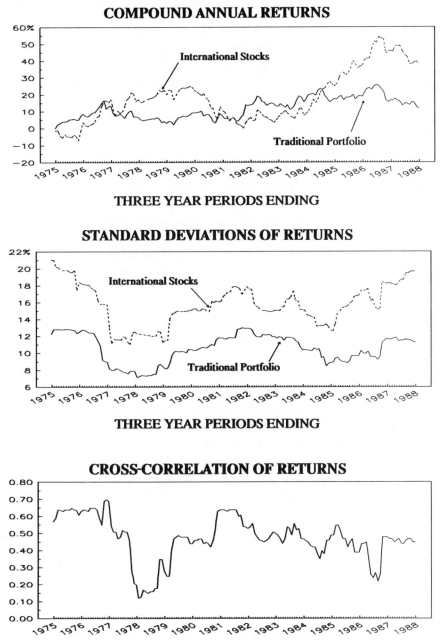

COMPOUND ANNUAL RETURNS

THREE YEAR PERIODS ENDING

STANDARD DEVIATIONS OF RETURNS

THREE YEAR PERIODS ENDING

CROSS-CORRELATION OF RETURNS

THREE YEAR PERIODS ENDING

Source: Based on data from Morgan Stanley Capital International Perspective and Roger G. Ibbotson and Rex. A. Sinquefield, *Stocks, Bonds, Bills and Inflation* (SBBI), 1982, updated in *SBBI 1989 Yearbook*, Ibbotson Associates, Chicago.

147

results in high transaction costs and significant delays in the settlement of security transactions. Foreign nations may suffer from political instability, which adds another dimension of risk to the investment management process. Foreign governments can also tax and/or in various ways restrict the flow of investment capital. Finally, the currency risk of a rising dollar can result in a poor dollar-dominated return, even though securities perform well in terms of their native currency. In essence, every foreign investment is two investments—one in the security itself, the other in the native foreign currency.

Despite these problems, international common stock investing is on the rise, and this trend will in all likelihood continue because of the increasing interdependence of the world's economies and the benefits to be derived from this important form of diversification.

INTERNATIONAL BONDS

Many of the arguments in favor of international stock investing apply to international bond investing as well. As with common stocks, the international bond market is larger than the U.S. bond market. International bonds provide returns that are competitive with U.S. bonds. But it is important to realize that the very high coupon returns from some international bonds are generally not fully realizable by U.S. investors. The "theory of interest rate parity" provides an explanation for this. It suggests that a higher foreign interest rate is often associated with a higher foreign inflation rate. This triggers a depreciation in the foreign currency relative to our dollar, thus impairing the realizable returns. In the end, an international bond's dollar-adjusted interest rate may not be as advantageous as the high coupon would indicate.

Figure 8–4 compares the compound annual returns, standard deviations, and cross-correlation of international bonds with the Traditional Portfolio for three-year periods from 1973 through 1988. The international bond index used in

FIGURE 8-4
International Bonds versus the Traditional Portfolio (1973–1988)

COMPOUND ANNUAL RETURNS

THREE YEAR PERIODS ENDING

STANDARD DEVIATIONS OF RETURNS

THREE YEAR PERIODS ENDING

CROSS-CORRELATION OF RETURNS

THREE YEAR PERIODS ENDING

Source: Based on data from Salomon Brothers, Inc. and Roger G. Ibbotson and Rex A. Sinquefield, *Stocks, Bonds, Bills and Inflation* (SBBI), 1982, updated in *SBBI 1989 Yearbook,* Ibbotson Associates, Chicago.

these graphs was provided by Salomon Brothers, Inc. The index measures the total return from a broad representation of international bonds from several foreign countries. Of particular interest is the low cross-correlation of returns that ranged from a low of $-.30$ to a high of .69. This would have provided a substantial diversification effect through the addition of international bonds to the Traditional Portfolio.

REAL ESTATE

Real estate is quite different from the other investment alternatives we have discussed. Each real estate property is unique in its geographic location, physical structure, tenant mix, and a variety of other attributes. The purchase and sale of real estate properties are negotiated transactions that can become very complex. Because the real estate market is composed of noninterchangeable, unique, illiquid properties, it is probably less efficient than the stock and bond markets. This inefficiency may give rise to exploitable opportunities for skilled investors to secure superior investment results. At the same time, however, the search and transaction costs involved with real estate investments are often high relative to other investment alternatives.

As an equity investment, real estate's capital appreciation has generally served as an effective hedge against inflation over long time horizons. Well-purchased real estate often also produces generous current cash flow. Many investors prefer to leverage their real estate investments with borrowed money. Although this increases the risk of the investment and diverts cash flow for debt service, it also magnifies the potential gains on the upside. Historically, tax benefits further enhanced the attractiveness of real estate investing. Unfortunately for the high-tax-bracket investor, the Tax Reform Act of 1986 largely eliminated real estate's favorable tax treatment. Despite this, real estate remains a major asset class which should be meaningfully represented in a well-diversified portfolio. Because each real estate investment is unique and illiquid, it is very important that real estate investments be adequately diversified. This can be accomplished by having ownership interests in different types of real estate investments such as office buildings, residential apartment complexes, shopping centers, and/or raw land in a variety of geographical locations.

Figure 8-5 compares the investment performance of real estate versus the Traditional Portfolio. The index used for real estate has been provided by CDA Investment Technologies, Inc. It represents the composite investment performance of the equity real estate separate accounts managed by several large insurance companies. The performance results reported by the insurance companies rely on an appraisal process of the current market values of the real estate properties in the separate accounts. By this measurement index, real estate produced returns that compared favorably with the Traditional Portfolio, but that had exceedingly little risk as measured by the standard deviation. The cross-correlation of returns between real estate and the Traditional Portfolio was usually negative, thus indicating a very strong diversification effect with the addition of real estate to the asset mix. There is considerable controversy over whether the appraisal process used to measure investment performance accurately reflects the actual variability of real estate values. My opinion is that the appraisal process understates the magnitude of changes in property values, and that the actual variability of return of real estate investments is much higher than is indicated by the standard deviation statistic. Likewise, although real estate probably has a low cross-correlation of return relative to the Traditional Portfolio, the appraisal process may result in statistics that overstate the diversification effect of including real estate in the asset mix.

In an attempt to get around the problems associated with an appraisal-process performance measurement, Figure 8-6 compares the investment performance of equity Real Estate Investment Trusts (REITS) with the Traditional Portfolio. Equity REITS are similar to closed-end funds of real estate properties. Like investment companies, they avoid corporate

FIGURE 8-5
Real Estate versus the Traditional Portfolio (1973–1988)

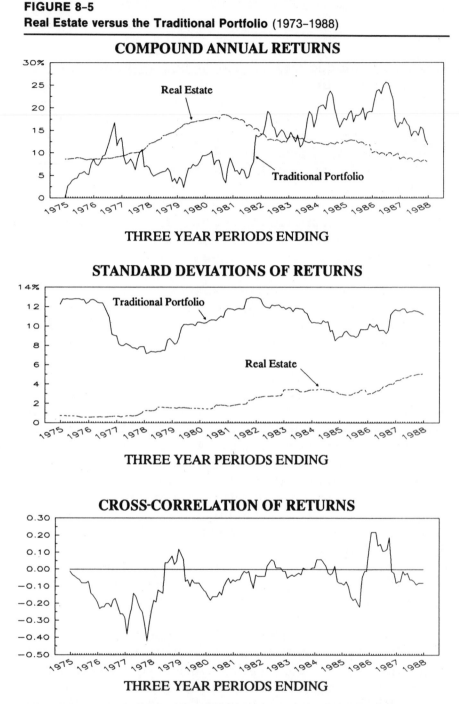

COMPOUND ANNUAL RETURNS

THREE YEAR PERIODS ENDING

STANDARD DEVIATIONS OF RETURNS

THREE YEAR PERIODS ENDING

CROSS-CORRELATION OF RETURNS

THREE YEAR PERIODS ENDING

Source: Based on data from CDA Investment Technologies, Inc. and Roger G. Ibbotson and Rex A. Sinquefield, *Stocks, Bonds, Bills and Inflation* (SBBI), 1982, updated in *SBBI 1989 Yearbook*, Ibbotson Associates, Chicago.

COMPOUND ANNUAL RETURNS

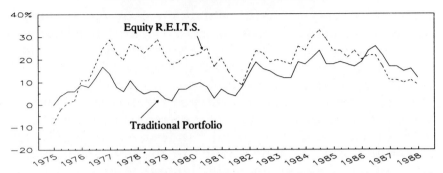

THREE YEAR PERIODS ENDING

STANDARD DEVIATIONS OF RETURNS

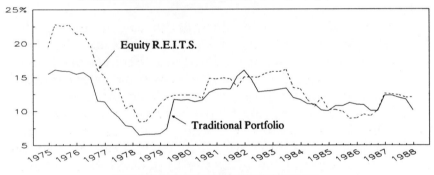

THREE YEAR PERIODS ENDING

CROSS-CORRELATION OF RETURNS

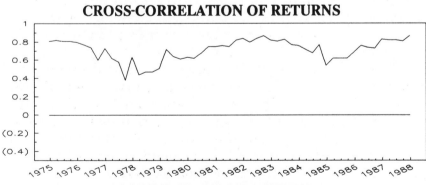

THREE YEAR PERIODS ENDING

Source: Based on data from National Association of Real Estate Investment Trusts, Inc. and Roger G. Ibbotson and Rex A. Sinquefield, *Stocks, Bonds, Bills and Inflation* (SBBI), 1982, updated in *SBBI 1989 Yearbook*, Ibbotson Associates, Chicago.

153

taxation by serving as a conduit for earnings on investments. The stocks of many equity REITS are traded on securities exchanges. This liquidity in trading activity provides
constant market consensus pricing of these investments. Although this eliminates the problems of an appraisal-driven
real estate performance measurement, it has the disadvantage of being an indirect form of ownership and therefore not
a "pure real estate investment." Indeed, equity REITS are
something of a "no man's land" in the investment world.
Real estate professionals claim ignorance about them because they trade like common stocks, while stock portfolio
managers often ignore them because they consider equity
REITS to be real estate investments rather than common
stocks!

Figure 8–6 shows that during the 16-year period 1973
through 1988, the returns of equity REITS usually dominated those of the Traditional Portfolio. (Because of the manner in which the performance statistics have been compiled,
the comparison has been done on a rolling calendar-quarter
basis rather than a rolling monthly basis.) The volatility of
equity REITS was on average higher than that of the Traditional Portfolio, and the cross-correlation of returns between
the two varied from a low of .38 to a high of .87. By stock market standards, equity REITS tend to generate above-average
yields and to have smaller capitalizations. For these reasons, the performance of equity REITS will not only be determined by the real estate market in general, but will also
be impacted by changes in interest rates and by the relative
performance of small company stocks.

Table 8–1 compares the compound annual returns and
standard deviations for all of the major investment alternatives for the 16-year time period beginning in 1973 and ending with 1988. The 16-year cross-correlation matrix is shown
for the same investment alternatives in Table 8–2. Let us
now compare the historical investment results of the Traditional Portfolio with a more broadly diversified approach
utilizing the additional investment alternatives we have reviewed in this chapter.

TABLE 8-1
Investment Performance Statistics for Major Asset Classes (1973-1988)

Asset Class	Compound Annual Return	Standard Deviation*
Treasury bills	8.1%	.8%
Corporate bonds	8.7	11.5
Common stocks	10.3	16.7
Small stocks	16.6	23.4
International stocks	16.1	17.2
International bonds	11.2	12.7
Equity REITS*	14.1	15.3
Real Estate	11.6	3.0

*The standard deviation statistic for equity REITS is based on quarterly return data. All other standard deviation statistics are based on monthly return data.

Source: Based on data from Roger G. Ibbotson and Rex A. Sinquefield, *Stocks, Bonds, Bills and Inflation* (SBBI), 1982, updated in *SBBI 1989 Yearbook*, Ibbotson Associates, Chicago; Morgan Stanley Capital International Perspective; Salomon Brothers, Inc.; National Association of Real Estate Investment Trusts, Inc.; and CDA Investment Technologies, Inc.

THE BROADLY DIVERSIFIED PORTFOLIO VERSUS THE TRADITIONAL PORTFOLIO

To construct the "Broadly Diversified Portfolio," we will utilize small stocks, international stocks, international bonds, and equity REITS in addition to the Traditional Portfolio's investment alternatives. (Equity REITS have been intentionally chosen as the real estate diversification alternative in order to not inadvertently build a case that overstates the benefits of diversification.) Table 8-3 shows the asset mix for each portfolio. The investment policy allocation of funds among short-term debt investments, long-term debt investments, and equity investments is the same for each portfolio in order to maintain comparability. Table 8-4 shows the historical compound annual return and standard deviation for each portfolio for the 10- and 16-year periods ending with 1988. Note that over both time periods, the Broadly Diver-

TABLE 8-2
Cross-correlation Matrix for Major Asset Classes (1973–1988)

	(1)	(2)	(3)	(4)	(5)	(6)	(7)	(8)
(1) Treasury bills	1.00							
(2) Corporate bonds	.05	1.00						
(3) Common stocks	−.09	.36	1.00					
(4) Small stocks	−.09	.22	.80	1.00				
(5) International stocks	−.16	.21	.52	.46	1.00			
(6) International bonds	−.12	.36	.11	.05	.63	1.00		
(7) Equity REITS*	−.11	.41	.76	.83	.65	.31	1.00	
(8) Real estate	.27	−.03	−.04	−.06	−.06	−.09	.00	1.00

*The cross-correlation statistics for equity REITS are based on quarterly return data. All other cross-correlation statistics are based on monthly return data.

Source: Based on data from Roger G. Ibbotson and Rex A. Sinquefield, *Stocks, Bonds, Bills and Inflation* (SBBI), 1982, updated in *SBBI 1989 Yearbook*, Ibbotson Associates, Chicago; Morgan Stanley Capital International Perspective; Salomon Brothers, Inc.; National Association of Real Estate Investment Trusts, Inc.; and CDA Investment Technologies, Inc.

TABLE 8-3
Traditional Portfolio versus Broadly Diversified Portfolio
Asset Mix Comparison

		Percentage Allocation	
Investment Policy Allocation	Asset Classes	Traditional Portfolio	Broadly Diversified Portfolio
10% Short-term debt investments	Treasury bills	10%	10%
40% Long-term debt investments	Long-term corporate bonds	40	20
	International bonds	0	20
50% Equity investments	S&P 500	50	15
	Small stocks	0	5
	International stocks	0	15
	Equity REITS	0	15
		100%	100%

TABLE 8-4
Comparative Investment Performance

	Traditional Portfolio	Broadly Diversified Portfolio
10-year Period Ending 1988		
Compound return	13.9%	15.3%
Standard deviation (risk)	12.0%	11.2%
Return per unit of risk*	1.2	1.4
16-year Period Ending 1988		
Compound return	9.9%	12.3%
Standard deviation (risk)	12.4%	11.5%
Return per unit of risk*	.8	1.1

*Calculated by dividing the compound return by the corresponding standard deviation.

Source: Based on data from Roger G. Ibbotson and Rex A. Sinquefield, *Stocks, Bonds, Bills and Inflation* (SBBI), 1982, updated in *SBBI 1989 Yearbook,* Ibbotson Associates, Chicago; Morgan Stanley Capital International Perspective; Salomon Brothers, Inc.; and National Association of Real Estate Investment Trusts, Inc.

sified Portfolio produced a higher compound annual return with less risk than the Traditional Portfolio.

Figure 8-7 compares the rolling three-year compound annual returns for the Broadly Diversified Portfolio versus the Traditional Portfolio. The Broadly Diversified Portfolio tended to dominate the Traditional Portfolio, but there also were prolonged periods of time when the reverse was true. This graph underscores the necessity of a long time horizon for evaluating the merits of a more broadly diversified investment strategy. Figure 8-8 shows the rolling three-year standard deviations of returns for both portfolios. The Broadly Diversified Portfolio usually had less risk. If we divide each portfolio's return by its standard deviation, we will have a summary statistic that can be used to evaluate returns on a risk-adjusted basis. Figure 8-9 plots this statistic for each portfolio. By this measure, the investment performance of the Broadly Diversified Portfolio dominated that of the Traditional Portfolio approximately 80 percent of the time.

Finally, Figure 8-10 shows the growth pattern of a $1.00 investment in each portfolio for the full 16-year period ending with 1988. For the first four years of this time period, the performance of the two portfolios tracked each other very closely. But during the last 12 years, the percentage gap widened significantly in favor of the Broadly Diversified Portfolio. By the end of the time horizon, a $1.00 investment in the Broadly Diversified Portfolio had grown to be worth $6.44—42 percent more than the $4.52 value for the Traditional Portfolio.

Of course, there is no guarantee that a more broadly diversified portfolio will result in better performance. If, for example, the U.S. dollar entered a prolonged period of strengthening relative to other currencies, the dollar-dominated investment performance from international stocks and bonds would be impaired. This could cause a traditionally diversified portfolio to outperform a more broadly diversified portfolio. Lacking any systematic way to confidently predict such events, however, more broadly diversified strategies are strongly favored.

Text continues on p. 164.

FIGURE 8-7
The Broadly Diversified Portfolio versus the Traditional Portfolio. Compound Annual Returns (1973–1988)

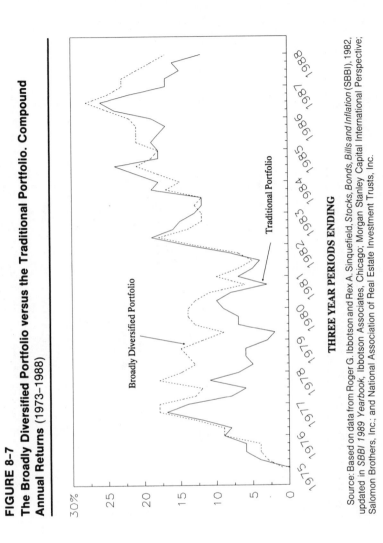

THREE YEAR PERIODS ENDING

Source: Based on data from Roger G. Ibbotson and Rex A. Sinquefield, *Stocks, Bonds, Bills and Inflation* (SBBI), 1982, updated in *SBBI 1989 Yearbook*, Ibbotson Associates, Chicago; Morgan Stanley Capital International Perspective; Salomon Brothers, Inc.; and National Association of Real Estate Investment Trusts, Inc.

FIGURE 8-8
The Broadly Diversified Portfolio versus the Traditional Portfolio. Standard Deviations of Returns (1973–1988)

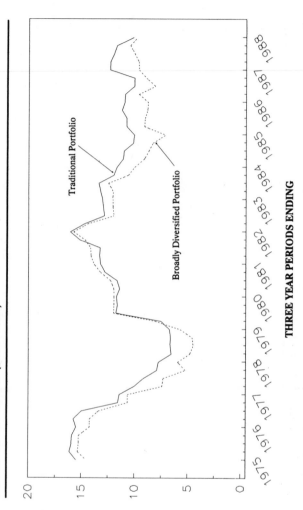

THREE YEAR PERIODS ENDING

Source: Based on data from Roger G. Ibbotson and Rex A. Sinquefield, *Stocks, Bonds, Bills and Inflation* (SBBI), 1982, updated in *SBBI 1989 Yearbook*, Ibbotson Associates, Chicago; Morgan Stanley Capital International Perspective; Salomon Brothers, Inc.; and National Association of Real Estate Investment Trusts, Inc.

FIGURE 8-9

The Broadly Diversified Portfolio versus the Traditional Portfolio. Compound Annual Returns per Unit of Risk (1973–1988)

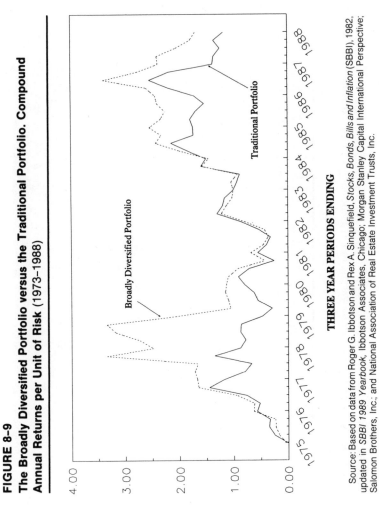

Source: Based on data from Roger G. Ibbotson and Rex A. Sinquefield, *Stocks, Bonds, Bills and Inflation* (SBBI), 1982, updated in *SBBI 1989 Yearbook*, Ibbotson Associates, Chicago; Morgan Stanley Capital International Perspective; Salomon Brothers, Inc.; and National Association of Real Estate Investment Trusts, Inc.

FIGURE 8-10
The Broadly Diversified Portfolio versus the Traditional Portfolio. Growth of $1.00 (1973–1988)

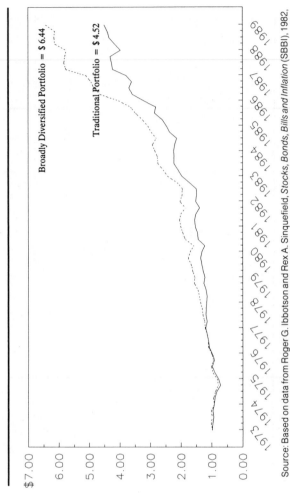

Broadly Diversified Portfolio = $ 6.44

Traditional Portfolio = $ 4.52

Source: Based on data from Roger G. Ibbotson and Rex A. Sinquefield, *Stocks, Bonds, Bills and Inflation* (SBBI), 1982, updated in *SBBI 1989 Yearbook*, Ibbotson Associates, Chicago; Morgan Stanley Capital International Perspective; Salomon Brothers, Inc.; and National Association of Real Estate Investment Trusts, Inc.

FIGURE 8-11

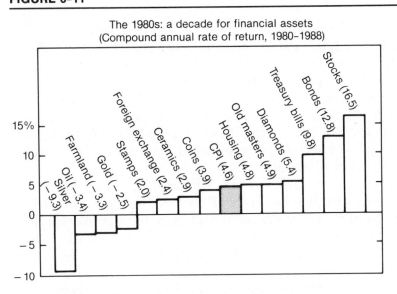

The 1980s: a decade for financial assets
(Compound annual rate of return, 1980–1988)

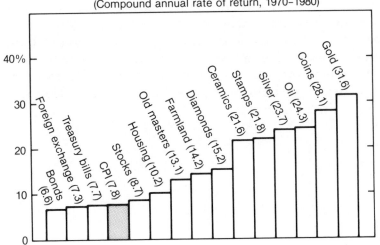

The 1970s: a decade for collectibles and commodities
(Compound annual rate of return, 1970–1980)

Source: © Salomon Brothers, Inc., 1987.

COLLECTIBLES AND COMMODITIES

With the exception of real estate, our discussion through-out this text has focused on financial assets. There are, of course, a wider variety of investment alternatives to consider, such as precious metals, stamps, coins, diamonds, and works of art. Figure 8-11 compares the investment performance of financial assets versus collectibles and commodities for the 1970s and 1980s. The exhibit suggests that tangible assets should be considered as potentially valuable diversification alternatives.

As with any investment alternative, tangible investments have drawbacks. They often have limited marketability and high transaction costs and may require special handling and care. Many of these tangible assets give their owners "nonpecuniary income" in the form of psychological pride of ownership. For this reason, investors who do not value this nonpecuniary income may in effect overpay for a tangible asset. This may explain why tangible investments are seldom used in institutional investment portfolios. Precious metal investments are probably the best diversification alternative for investors who want to allocate a portion of their portfolio to tangible investments, but who do not have the interest or expertise to become knowledgeable collectors. Although precious metal returns are quite volatile, over the long term they may help hedge against both inflation and economic/political uncertainty.

CHAPTER 9

PORTFOLIO OPTIMIZATION

All business proceeds on beliefs, on judgments of
probabilities and not on certainties.
—*Charles W. Eliot* (1834–1926)

This chapter is devoted to a discussion of portfolio optimization. It may be particularly valuable to readers who are interested in, or intend to use, computer programs that are designed to identify optimal asset allocations for various client situations. Those readers who are not interested in this technical aspect of asset allocation may want to proceed to Chapter 10.

In Chapter 7 we learned that there are good and bad ways to allocate assets in constructing investment portfolios. Good asset allocations are said to be *efficient*. With an efficient asset mix, the portfolio's expected return is maximized subject to a specific portfolio risk level. Bad asset allocations are said to be *inefficient*. With inefficient portfolios, it is possible to increase the portfolio's expected return without increasing portfolio risk (or equivalently, to reduce portfolio risk without sacrificing the portfolio's expected return) by simply reallocating funds among the various investment positions. Each asset in a portfolio contributes to both the portfolio's expected return and its risk. For a given level of portfolio risk, an inefficient portfolio has some assets that make higher risk-adjusted incremental contributions to portfolio return than other assets.

For example, if the international bonds in a portfolio contribute more incremental portfolio return per unit of portfolio risk than do small stocks, then we can improve the portfolio's return without increasing portfolio risk by simply selling some small stock holdings to provide additional funds for international bond investments. Because such a swap changes the composition of the portfolio, each asset's risk-adjusted contribution to portfolio return also changes, and therefore needs to be recalculated. If we again find differences in the risk-adjusted incremental contributions to portfolio return for the various assets, the portfolio's return can be further improved (without increasing portfolio risk) by swapping some of the asset that now makes the smallest risk-adjusted contribution to portfolio return for some of the asset that makes the largest contribution. If we continue in this manner, we will eventually run out of advantageous swaps. The resulting asset mix maximizes the expected return for that particular level of portfolio risk. Hence, the portfolio is efficient. As a condition of that efficiency, each asset's risk-adjusted incremental contribution to the portfolio's expected return is equal. (If this were not true, we could obviously continue to improve the portfolio's expected return without increasing portfolio risk by engaging in more swaps.) By analogy, you know that you are standing on the top of a mountain (i.e., you have maximized your altitude) when you lose altitude regardless of which direction you walk. Similarly, an efficient portfolio is like being at the top of the mountain, in that the pursuit of any alternative asset allocation with equivalent portfolio risk will result in a loss of portfolio expected return.

For any given set of investment alternatives, there is a unique efficient portfolio that corresponds to a given level of portfolio risk. The collection of all efficient portfolios corresponding to the full range of portfolio risk possibilities is known as the *efficient frontier*. Although all efficient portfolios on the efficient frontier are good because they maximize expected return for any given level of risk, from a particular client's point of view they are not equally desirable. The reason is that people vary in their risk tolerance. The optimal portfolio for a client is that unique portfolio on the efficient frontier which maximizes the client's return subject to his particular level of risk tolerance.

With the aid of computers utilizing sophisticated quadratic programming techniques, it is possible to mathematically identify the asset allocations that correspond to each portfolio lying on the efficient frontier. These computer optimization programs require as inputs, estimates of expected returns and standard deviations for each investment alternative, as well as estimates of the cross-correlation of returns among all of the investment alternatives. Hopefully, the discussions we have had thus far have underscored the dangers of blindly using historical data to derive estimates of these variables. The fact that measures of uncertainty are incorporated into the inputs does not eliminate this danger. The difficulties are further compounded by the sensitivity of output to small variations in the input variables. The admonition often given to students in introductory computer programming courses is particularly relevant here: "GIGO (garbage in, garbage out)!"

As a practical matter, most professionals who are experienced with optimization programs use historical cross-correlations and standard deviations as a departure point for developing estimates of future correlations and standard deviations. Historical returns, however, are of much less value in estimating future returns. For example, for the 20-year period ending with 1988, common stocks had a compound annual return that was only 2 percent greater than that of Treasury bills. Given the much greater risk of common stocks, we would certainly expect common stocks to outperform Treasury bills in the future by a spread much larger than 2 percent. One way around this problem is to use longer term historical relationships among asset class returns to develop estimates of future expected returns.

Another approach utilizes the implications of modern portfolio theory to derive estimates of the expected returns for various asset classes. For example, modern portfolio theory suggests that it is optimal for an average risk investor to hold an investment portfolio that has an asset mix that mirrors the percentage allocation of assets of the world investable capital market. The estimation procedure first uses historical data as a basis for developing estimates of the standard deviations and cross-correlations for the various asset classes. Then the allocation of the world investable capital market is determined. (For example, see Figure 1-1, which shows an estimate of this allocation as of December 31, 1988.) Under an assumption that this asset mix is optimal for an average risk investor, it is possible to work backwards to solve for the expected return of each asset class.

Once the inputs for expected return, standard deviation, and cross-correlation have been estimated for the asset classes, it is a straightforward, although sophisticated, mathematical calculation to derive the asset allocations for portfolios on the efficient frontier. It is then necessary to select the specific portfolio along the efficient frontier that is most appropriate for the client in question. One method for doing this is to describe the risk/return characteristics of a representative sample of portfolios from the efficient frontier and then have the client choose which he likes best. The client's choice will be an indirect indication of his risk tolerance. Because there is no way to directly measure a client's risk tolerance, this process of choosing an optimal portfolio will always have a subjective dimension.

Many computer optimization programs have a built-in feature that selects the optimal portfolio based on an input-variable that attempts to describe a client's risk tolerance. To do this, the computer identifies the efficient portfolio that optimizes the portfolio's "utility" for the investor. *Utility* is an expression borrowed from economic theory which loosely translated means "psychological satisfaction." In an optimization program, utility is calculated as the portfolio's expected return minus a risk penalty. The risk penalty in turn is a function of two things: the portfolio's risk, which can be mathematically quantified, and the client's risk tolerance, which can be only subjectively estimated. To indirectly assess a client's risk tolerance, some computer optimization programs utilize a decision-making procedure like the one we developed in Chapter 6, which requires the investor to choose a preferred portfolio allocation between Treasury bills and the S&P 500. The percentage allocated to the S&P 500 serves as the input value for the investor's risk-tolerance variable. For example, a risk-tolerance input of 80 corresponds to a preferred 80 percent commitment to the S&P 500, and hence indicates high risk tolerance, whereas a risk-tolerance input of 25 corresponds to a preferred S&P 500 commitment of 25 percent, which indicates low risk tolerance.

The portfolio optimization program used in the next section uses an alternative approach. The client is asked to specify how much additional return over Treasury bill yields he would require to actively choose a 50 percent Treasury bill/50 percent S&P 500 portfolio balance. An investor with low risk tolerance, for example, might require the S&P 500 to have an expected return that is 20 percent higher than Treasury bills in order to actively choose a 50/50 portfolio balance. The risk-tolerance input variable would therefore have a value of 20. A higher risk-tolerance investor may require the S&P 500 to have an expected return only 3 percent higher than Treasury bills to actively choose a 50/50 portfolio balance. The risk-tolerance input variable would in this case be assigned a value of 3.

COMPUTER OPTIMIZATION PROGRAMS

Let us now observe a computer optimization program in action.[1] Table 9-1 shows the input values for each asset class. As we discussed previously, historical data is less helpful in deriving estimates of expected returns than it is for estimating standard deviations and cross-correlations. For this reason, more judgment has been exercised in developing expected return estimates. For Treasury bills and corporate bonds, the yields to maturity for each asset class are used as estimates for expected returns. A dividend discount model is used to derive the expected return for common stocks. Although international stocks and bonds outperformed their domestic counterparts by a wide margin during the recent

---

[1]All computer optimizations were performed on Vestek Systems, Inc. software.

TABLE 9-1
Computer Optimization Program Input Values

Expected Return Input Value	Standard Deviation Input Value	Asset Class	Cross-correlation Matrix Input Value							
			(1)	(2)	(3)	(4)	(5)	(6)	(7)	(8)
5.8%	.3%	(1) Treasury bills	1.00							
10.1%	11.7%	(2) Corporate bonds	.06	1.00						
12.3%	17.1%	(3) Common stocks	-.09	.35	1.00					
14.5%	24.0%	(4) Small stocks	-.09	.21	.80	1.00				
13.3%	17.7%	(5) Int'l. stocks	-.15	.22	.52	.46	1.00			
10.1%	12.3%	(6) Int'l. bonds	-.16	.37	.12	.05	.63	1.00		
14.5%	15.6%	(7) Equity REITS	-.10	.41	.77	.85	.66	.33	1.00	
11.2%	1.8%	(8) Real estate	.45	-.09	-.03	.00	-.09	-.08	.06	1.00

past, part of that performance margin was attributable to a weakening of the dollar relative to international currencies. For these illustrations, we will not presume that this trend will continue. Accordingly, the expected return for international bonds is estimated to be the same as that for domestic corporate bonds. Given the higher economic growth rates in some other parts of the world, however, the expected return for international stocks is estimated to be slightly higher than domestic stocks. Because equity REITS have small stock characteristics, they are assigned a similar expected return.

The standard deviation and cross-correlation estimates are based primarily on historical data.[2] Some adjustments had to be made in the standard deviation and cross-correlation inputs for equity REITS because the performance data was available on only a quarterly basis, whereas other asset classes had monthly data. The standard deviation for Treasury bills is also adjusted downward in order to compensate for the tendency of this asset class' volatility to be overstated by its drifting mean.

Assume we have a client with whom we have thoroughly reviewed the concept of time horizon and he understands the risk/return characteristics of Treasury bills and the S&P 500. We describe to him a portfolio composed of 50 percent Treasury bills and 50 percent S&P 500 and ask him this question: "With Treasury bills currently yielding 5.8 percent, how much additional expected return would you require from common stocks in order for you to actively choose a portfolio allocation of 50 percent Treasury bills/50 percent S&P 500?" The client's response will be an indirect measure of his risk tolerance and will give us a value for the "risk premium" input variable to the computer optimization program. For our example optimizations, we will assume that the client has responded that he would require common stocks to have an expected return of 15.8 percent—10 percent more than

---

[2]These statistics do not match those described in Chapter 8 because they pertain to a different time period and in some situations use different data series.

Treasury bills' expected return of 5.8 percent. Based on a long-term historical equity risk premium of between 6 and 7 percent, a risk premium value of 10 indicates a relatively low-risk tolerance.

Table 9–2 shows the asset allocation computer output for five different optimizations. In each case, the computer identifies the optimal portfolio (based on the input variables and any specified constraints) for a client whose risk tolerance corresponds to a risk premium of 10 percent. The first optimization is unconstrained in that anywhere from 0 percent to 100 percent of the portfolio can be committed to any of the eight asset classes. Based on the inputs, the optimal portfolio would have an asset allocation of 20.5 percent equity REITS and 79.5 percent real estate. The portfolio's expected return would be 11.9 percent with a standard deviation of 3.6 percent. There would be better than a 99.9 percent probability that this allocation will have a positive return during the following year.

Does this allocation make good sense? Yes, given the inputs. Real estate's expected return input is high relative to a quite low standard deviation input. Similarly, the equity REITS asset class has a very high expected return input with a relatively modest standard deviation input. These two asset classes would also combine to produce strong portfolio diversification effect given a cross-correlation of return input value of .06. Any alteration in the allocation between these two asset classes or the inclusion of any additional asset classes would produce a portfolio with less desirable risk/return characteristics for this particular client.

Now, would we recommend this portfolio to our client? Perhaps we would, if we had extremely high confidence in all of our data inputs. Is there a basis for such confidence? The standard deviation input value for the real estate asset class is based on an appraisal process that quite likely understates real estate's actual volatility. (Just because you cannot see the volatility of a nonliquid investment, that does not mean the volatility is not there.) It is also unsettling to note that the cross-correlation measure of .06 between equity REITS and real estate indicates that the returns of these two asset

TABLE 9-2
Optimization Results and Sensitivity Analysis for a Client Who Specifies a Risk Premium of 10.0%*

Asset Class	1 All 8 Asset Classes	2 7 Asset Classes	3 Expected Return of Equity REITS Decreased by 1%	4 Standard Deviation of Equity REITS Increased by 1%	5 Equity REITS Perfectly Correlated with Small Stocks
(1) Treasury bills	0.0%	23.8%	26.1%	27.4%	0.9%
(2) Corporate bonds	0.0	15.2	21.0	18.4	20.2
(3) Common stocks	0.0	0.0	1.8	0.0	0.0
(4) Small stocks	0.0	0.0	0.5	0.0	0.0
(5) International stocks	0.0	0.0	8.2	4.4	0.0
(6) International bonds	0.0	18.2	14.8	16.0	31.2
(7) Equity REITS	20.5	42.8	27.6	33.8	47.7
(8) Real estate	79.5	-	-	-	-
	100.0%	100.0%	100.0%	100.0%	100.0%
Portfolio Characteristics					
Expected Return	11.9%	11.0%	10.2%	10.6%	12.2%
Standard Deviation	3.6%	8.7%	8.0%	8.3%	9.6%
Probability of achieving a positive return	99.9%	90.2%	90.4%	90.3%	90.3%

*The optimization results shown have been produced using Vestek Systems, Inc. software.

classes are uncorrelated! To the extent to which we lack confidence in our inputs, we should likewise lack confidence in our output. Given the inputs, it is not surprising that the optimal allocation for the client is extremely heavily oriented toward real estate. Rather than concluding from the output that a portfolio heavily oriented to real estate is best for the client, it may be more appropriate to consider the output as a warning signal to not take the input values too seriously.

Given that a strong likelihood exists that the actual risk of real estate is misrepresented by the appraisal-driven standard deviation statistic, we could choose to simply eliminate it as an asset class and rely on equity REITS to be an alternate proxy for real estate as an asset class. Optimization 2 in Table 9–2 does just that by constraining the allocation to real estate to 0 percent. For the same client, the optimal portfolio is now shifted heavily toward a 42.8 percent equity REITS allocation with the remainder of the portfolio allocated to Treasury bills, corporate bonds, and international bonds. This portfolio's expected return of 11.0 percent is lower than the first portfolio's, and its standard deviation of 8.7 percent is much higher. (Note that if we hold the risk premium input constant at 10 percent the optimal portfolio under alternative input assumptions will have varying risk levels. That is because the optimal portfolio expresses a risk/return trade-off that results in different optimal portfolio risk levels as inputs are modified.) With this portfolio, we have a 90.2 percent probability of achieving a positive return during the following year.

We can be somewhat more comfortable with this portfolio, because it is better diversified than portfolio 1. At the same time it is troubling to see that three major asset classes (common stocks, small stocks, and international stocks) are completely unrepresented while more than 40 percent of the portfolio is committed to equity REITS. Is this high commitment to equity REITS warranted? Again, it is really a question of how much confidence we have in the input variables for the various asset classes. Optimizations 1 and 2 estimate that equity REITS have an expected return of 14.5 percent with a standard deviation of 15.6 percent. This indicates that there are two chances out of three that equity REITS will give us a return during the following year of between −1.1 percent and 30.1 percent (i.e., 14.5 percent +/−15.6 percent). Not a very specific estimate, is it?

Let us engage in some sensitivity analysis. Assume that our estimate of the standard deviation is perfectly accurate, but that we have slightly overstated the expected return for equity REITS by 1 percent. The "true" typical range of returns is therefore between −2.1 percent and 29.1 percent (i.e., 13.5 percent +/−15.6 percent). For all practical purposes, this does not appear to be a significant change in the estimated performance characteristics of equity REITS. If we revise the input for the expected return of equity REITS down by 1 percent while keeping all other data inputs constant, what effect will this have on the output? Optimization 3 in Table 9-2 describes the asset allocation performance characteristics of the revised optimal portfolio. Note how this very minor change in one input variable radically alters the allocation among the asset classes. The commitment to equity REITS drops dramatically from 42.8 percent to 27.6 percent with small positions established for the previously unrepresented asset classes of common stocks, small stocks, and international stocks. As expected, the portfolio expected return drops, but the portfolio standard deviation is lower as well. The likelihood of portfolio 3 producing a positive one-year return is 90.4 percent.

For optimization 4, instead of measuring the impact of using a lower estimate of the expected return for equity REITS, we increase the estimate of the standard deviation for equity REITS by 1 percent, from 15.6 percent to 16.6 percent. In every other respect, the input variables are identical to those for optimization 2. Again, this very minor revision in one input variable triggers a pronounced redistribution of assets in forming a revised optimal portfolio. The equity REITS commitment drops from 42.8 percent to 33.8 percent with the difference reallocated to Treasury bills, corporate bonds, and international stocks. Both the expected return and the risk of this revised portfolio are lower than that of portfolio 2. The probability that portfolio 4 will produce a positive one-year return is 90.3 percent.

There is one more dimension along which we can alter the input data for equity REITS—its cross-correlation relative to other asset classes. By examining the cross-correlation matrix in Table 9-1, we can see that equity REITS have their highest correlation with the small stocks asset class. For optimization 5, it is assumed that the cross-correlation between equity REITS and small stocks is one of perfect positive correlation (i.e., no diversification effect between the two asset classes). The cross-correlation of returns between equity REITS and every other asset class therefore will be changed to match the cross-correlation pattern of small stocks versus the other asset classes. All other input variables are identical to those for optimization 2. This time, the major changes are an almost complete elimination of Treasury bills and a substantially higher allocation to international bonds. The equity REITS commitment increases to nearly 50 percent of portfolio assets. As is the case with portfolio 2, there is no commitment to common stocks, small stocks, or international stocks. Of the five optimizations, this portfolio has the highest expected return as well as the highest risk. The probability of portfolio 5 producing a positive one-year return is 90.3 percent.

The sensitivity analysis we performed with optimizations 3, 4, and 5 should convince anyone that the output is indeed very sensitive to minor changes in the input variables, which themselves are extremely difficult to estimate. This argues for an approach that constrains the propensity for computer optimization programs to make extreme allocations to various asset classes.

For the final optimization, we will begin by specifying that a core 40 percent of the portfolio will be allocated among Treasury bills, corporate bonds, and the S&P 500 in the same proportions that constitute the Traditional Portfolio discussed in Chapter 8. Other constraints are that each asset class must have allocations of not less than 5 percent nor more than 25 percent of portfolio assets. This approach blends aspects of the Traditional Portfolio balance with constrained minimum/maximum allocations for all seven asset classes, thus insuring breadth of diversification. Table 9–3 shows the range of permissible portfolio commitments to each asset class and the asset allocation for this constrained optimization. By summing the minimum holdings for the asset classes, we see that the constraints operate to prespecify 61 percent of the portfolio. The other 39 percent of assets are optimized subject to the constraints.

If we compare this constrained portfolio to portfolio 2, which uses the same input variables without constraints, we see that the constraints have triggered a loss of .2 percent in the portfolio's expected return, with an increase in portfolio risk of .3 percent. But in exchange, we have a much

TABLE 9–3
Constrained Optimization Results for a Client Who Specifies a Risk Premium of 10.0%*

		Permissible Range	
	Constrained Optimal Allocation	Minimum Holding	Maximum Holding
Asset Class			
Treasury bills	18.1%	5.0%	25.0%
Corporate bonds	16.0%	16.0%	25.0%
Common stocks	20.0%	20.0%	25.0%
Small stocks	5.0%	5.0%	25.0%
International stocks	5.0%	5.0%	25.0%
International bonds	21.4%	5.0%	25.0%
Equity REITS	14.5%	5.0%	25.0%
	100.0%	61.0%	
Portfolio Characteristics			
Expected return	10.8%		
Standard deviation	9.0%		
Probability of achieving a positive return	88.8%		

*The optimization results shown have been produced using Vestek Systems, Inc. software.

more broadly diversified and well-balanced portfolio with 30 percent of the assets now allocated to the otherwise unrepresented asset classes: common stocks, small stocks and international stocks. Although this constrained portfolio is mathematically suboptimal relative to the unconstrained portfolio, the benefits of diversification are still largely retained. For example, Table 9-3 indicates that the constrained portfolio has a standard deviation of 9.0 percent based on the historical cross-correlation of returns among asset classes. If the asset classes were perfectly positively correlated, however, the standard deviation would be 12.3 percent—a risk level that is over one third higher. Given the difficulties in deriving good estimates for each input variable, and the sensitivity of computer output to small changes in the input variables, the constrained portfolio allocation shown in Table 9-3 is a much more sensible recommendation for the client than the unconstrained portfolio allocation shown in Table 9-2 for optimization 2.

Consider an efficient mix of Treasury bills, bonds, and stocks that has maximized the portfolio expected return subject to a portfolio standard deviation of 12 percent. Now let us permit investment in a fourth asset class, for example, real estate. Depending on the risk/return characteristics of real estate, we may find a new asset allocation using all four asset classes which produces a higher maximum portfolio expected return consistent with a portfolio standard deviation of 12 percent. Assume that the optimal real estate allocation for this four-asset-class portfolio is 30 percent of assets. Do we get the same increase in portfolio return from the first half of our optimal 30 percent commitment (as we increase the real estate allocation from 0 percent to 15 percent) as we do with the second half of our commitment (as we continue to increase the real estate allocation from 15 percent to 30 percent)? In other words, does the portfolio return increase linearly with an increase in the real estate commitment until the optimal allocation is reached, or does the impact on portfolio return change as we incrementally increase the size of the allocation?

We can answer this by performing a series of constrained optimizations that plot the returns associated with efficient portfolios with varying real estate commitments. If graphed, the relationship between portfolio expected return and the percentage real estate commitment might look like that shown in Figure 9-1. Note that the shape of the curve is steeper as real estate is first introduced into the asset mix. This indicates that at first the impact on the portfolio return is high as real estate diversification begins. As the real estate commitment increases toward its optimal allocation of 30 percent of assets, the portfolio return continues to increase, *but it does so at a diminishing rate.* The curve is relatively flat at and around the optimal allocation of 30

FIGURE 9-1

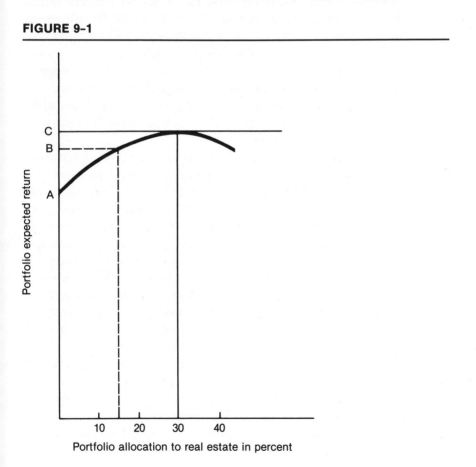

percent. This indicates that varying the size of the real estate commitment by a few percentage points on either side of the optimal 30 percent commitment has a relatively small impact on the portfolio expected return. Beyond 30 percent, an increase in the real estate commitment reduces portfolio return slowly at first, then at a faster rate.

Point A corresponds to the maximum expected return possible for a portfolio with a standard deviation equal to 12 percent when investment choices are constrained to only Treasury bills, bonds, and stocks. Point C corresponds to the maximum expected return possible utilizing real estate in addition to the other three asset classes. The distance AC is therefore the improvement in portfolio return made possible by the optimal allocation of real estate in the asset mix. Point B corresponds to the maximum return possible if the portfolio is constrained to a 15 percent real estate commitment. We can clearly see that most of the increase in the portfolio expected return is obtained by changing the allocation from 0 percent to 15 percent, with a much smaller increase produced by changing the real estate commitment from 15 percent to 30 percent.

This fact has very important investment implications. First, it removes some of the anxiety of trying to find the exact asset allocation that will maximize the risk-adjusted portfolio return. In utilizing an asset allocation computer program, we know that we can have only limited confidence in our estimates of expected returns, standard deviations, and cross-correlations used as input variables. Correspondingly, we can have only limited confidence in the optimal asset allocation generated as the output. We also know how even slight changes in the input variables result in rather drastic shifts in the portfolio asset allocation. Although at first this may seem to be somewhat discouraging, it has a bright flip side. It means that rather significant shifts of assets around the optimal mix may produce surprisingly little impact on the portfolio's risk/return characteristics. Thus, there may be a range of alternative asset allocations that produces similar, but not identical, portfolio risk/return characteristics.

For example, we previously performed an unconstrained optimization to identify the best asset allocation for a low-risk-tolerance client. (Refer to optimization 2 in Table 9–2.) Although we knew we had the mathematically correct answer given the inputs, it was uncomfortable to see that three major asset classes were completely unrepresented in his recommended asset allocation. By constraining the optimization program to maintain minimum allocations across all asset classes, we derived an alternative asset allocation that had portfolio risk/return characteristics almost as attractive as the unconstrained alternative. For a passive asset allocation investor, who believes it is impossible to engage successfully in market timing, it is obviously advisable to hold the more broadly diversified portfolio, even though it is not quite mathematically optimal based on the inputs. The justification for choosing the mathematically less than optimal asset mix stems from a realistic acknowledgment of the limited confidence we should have in the output.

Although it is true that a variety of asset allocations may have similar portfolio expected risk/return characteristics, after the fact the results will vary widely. This variance is expected and, for the passive asset allocation investor, reflects the chance element inherent in investing. For those who want to minimize the impact of chance (i.e., minimize the potential impact of both good luck and bad luck), the more broadly diversified alternatives are recommended.

The implications are no less important to an active asset allocation investor who wants to engage in market timing. For example, it may be possible to design a portfolio with a restricted range of portfolio allocations between two market-timed asset classes. As long as the range is not too wide and is centered near the optimal allocation, then the portfolio expected risk/return characteristics for the various allocations will be similar along this range. In essence, by maintaining a core diversified portfolio, a market timer can maintain most of the advantages of diversification while still providing an opportunity for superior market timing judgment to produce value-added incremental returns.

Psychologically, it is easy to believe that a precise answer is more certain and therefore deserves a higher level of confidence than an approximate answer. For example, assume that an investor wants advice concerning what portion of his portfolio to commit to international stocks. For guidance, he decides to consult two different investment advisers. The first adviser recommends exactly 19.3 percent of assets. The second adviser recommends about 20 percent of assets. Even though there is no real difference in the recommended size of the allocation, isn't there a tendency for the investor to have more confidence in the first adviser's recommendation because it is more specific?

Computer optimization programs give asset allocation recommendations that are as precise as those of the first adviser. In addition, optimization programs can specify precise probability estimates of achieving various levels of return during different holding periods and format this information in either tabular or graphic form, with or without color pie charts! All this technology can be seductive to both investment advisers and their clients. Unfortunately, there is also a corresponding opportunity for uninformed or unscrupulous investment advisers to encourage clients to blindly follow the "objective recommendations" generated by the technology. Knowledgeable investment advisers will maintain proper perspective by keeping in mind that input variables are hard to specify with any degree of confidence and that the output of optimization programs is highly sensitive to small changes in the input variables. Computer programs cannot eliminate the uncertainty inherent in investing. Thoughtful consideration of the output makes this clear. For example, if the standard deviation of an optimized portfolio is 19 percent, what value is there in knowing that the portfolio's expected return is not 12 percent, but rather is exactly 12.23 percent?!

Despite their limitations, computer asset allocation programs are powerful tools which can be of great value in the money management process if used properly. They quickly and accurately perform very complex mathematical calculations that are useful in portfolio-sensitivity analysis and the comparison of alternative "what if" scenarios. Many commercially available programs have features that also take into consideration such factors as transaction costs and the impact of income taxes. As an additional tool available to investment advisers, optimization programs improve the thought and decision-making process by pointing a finger in the direction of alternative asset allocations that may be better suited to the realization of client objectives. They are also of significant educational value in providing clients with a better understanding of the probable performance results associated with alternative strategies.

CHAPTER 10

KNOWING YOUR CLIENT

The beginning is the most important part of the
work.
                        —*Plato* (circa 428–348 B.C.)
                                        Republic

Money is paper blood.
                        —Attributed to *Bob Hope* (1903-   )

We will now turn to a discussion of how to apply the ideas
we have developed thus far to the dynamics of an ongoing
client-adviser relationship. Figure 10-1 is a flow chart that
describes the steps of the money management process as an
interactive loop that continually feeds back into itself. Each
of these steps will be discussed in detail in Chapters 10
through 12.

The first two steps, which we will cover in this chapter,
are the foundation of the money management process and
can be grouped together under the heading *Knowing your
client*. The next three steps consist of *Managing client expectations*. The positioning of this group of three steps is crucial. They build directly on the foundation of *Knowing your
client*, and out of necessity *precede* the last three steps which
constitute what we typically consider to be *Money management*. The process of managing client expectations is as important to the long-term realization of client objectives as is
the process of actually managing the money. Many clients
fail to reach their objectives as a result of simply not adhering to a sensible long-term strategy. Often this can be
traced to unrealistic expectations. In essence, it is not enough

FIGURE 10–1
Money Management Process

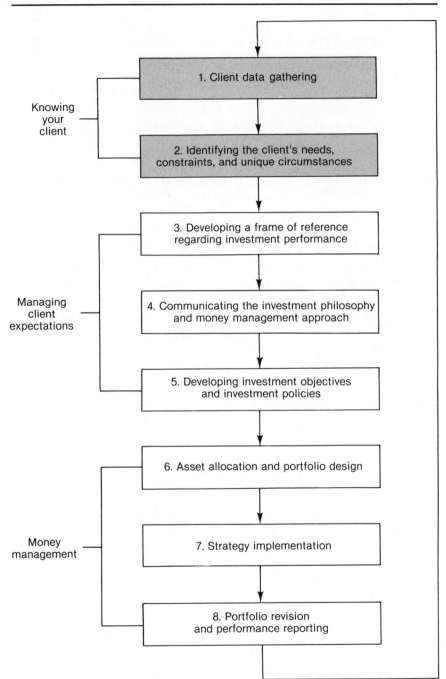

Knowing your client

1. Client data gathering

2. Identifying the client's needs, constraints, and unique circumstances

Managing client expectations

3. Developing a frame of reference regarding investment performance

4. Communicating the investment philosophy and money management approach

5. Developing investment objectives and investment policies

Money management

6. Asset allocation and portfolio design

7. Strategy implementation

8. Portfolio revision and performance reporting

for an adviser to be properly managing a client's portfolio. It is also crucial that the client *understand* that the portfolio is being properly managed. Without that understanding, it is unlikely that a client will be able to adhere to an appropriate long-term strategy throughout the pressures of extreme market conditions.

It is interesting to note that money is not actually invested until the next to last step in this flow chart. Unfortunately, many clients view the first five steps of this process as requiring too much time and effort on their part. They prefer to limit their involvement to the initial selection of a money manager who in turn has full reponsibility to handle the last three steps of designing the portfolio asset allocation, implementing strategy, and providing feedback. Many investment advisers are likewise too quick to shortcut the process and jump immediately to the last three steps. The likelihood of a client's reaching his objectives, however, is greatly enhanced by resisting the temptation to take shortcuts. Although this eight-step process requires the thoughtful commitment of both adviser and client, it can be effectively and efficiently accomplished within a relatively short period of time. The first two steps will be covered in this chapter. The remaining steps will be discussed in the next two chapters.

STEP 1: CLIENT DATA GATHERING

The client may be an individual, a couple, or small institutional account such as a trusteed retirement plan, endowment, or foundation. Regardless of the type of client however, the goal of the data-gathering process is to "know the client." Much of the data is factual or quantitative in nature. Beyond this is a realm of more subjective qualitative information, which attempts to assess what it is like "inside the client's skin."

Advisers who prefer to delegate the data-gathering process to a support person may be doing themselves and their clients a disservice. It is important for data gathering to be handled by the adviser with face-to-face interaction with the client. The psychological bonding between client and adviser begins here and helps to establish a sense of comfort which is important given the magnitude of the investment decisions to be made. The client also has the opportunity to begin to understand how the adviser thinks, and certainly the adviser will gain a level of understanding of the client which goes beyond the facts and figures written down in a data questionnaire.

Be alert for clues regarding the client's *present* risk tolerance. The word *present* is italicized because as we discussed previously, risk tolerance is subject to modification within a rather broad range, based on providing your client with a framework for informed decision making. Without directly asking for risk-tolerance information, much can be inferred from the current composition of the portfolio. If the client usually holds 90 percent of his portfolio in money market funds and bank CDs, it is a strong indication that he may be quite risk-averse. Another client who holds a disproportionately large portion of his portfolio in gold bullion, rare coins, diamonds and other hard assets is likewise telling you something about his present investment attitudes. Occasionally, contradictory impressions emerge. For example, a person who describes himself as being very risk-averse may have a large portfolio commitment to a small company traded over-the-counter. By eliciting more information it is learned that the stock was inherited from his mother who was the company's founder. This information is important because of the psychological/emotional dimension of the decision-making process regarding retention or sale of this stock. When listing your client's assets and liabilities, it is helpful to organize the balance sheet in a format that supports the investment decision-making process. The following classifications are recommended:

1. Short-term debt investments.
2. Long-term debt investments.
3. Equity investments.
4. Lifestyle assets.
5. Liabilities.

As we concluded in Chapter 6, the most important decision a client makes is the balance chosen between interest-generating assets and equity assets. This balance determines the risk/return characteristics of the portfolio. By gathering data in the format recommended, the current portfolio balance can be quickly assessed. Lifestyle assets include home and personal property, as well as vacation homes. Occasionally, a client objects to the classification of a vacation home as a lifestyle asset, but unless it produces a positive cash flow by generating rental income in excess of the expenses of ownership it should probably be considered a user of wealth, not a producer of wealth.

The balance between investment assets and lifestyle assets provides one indication of the client's financial discipline and thrift. More information can be inferred from an analysis of his cash flow. How much of his income is absorbed in lifestyle expenditures versus committed to building investment net worth?

Because many investment assets generate taxable income, a client's personal income tax return is a useful source of information to double-check that all assets and liabilities have been accounted for.

The data-gathering process also provides a valuable opportunity to assess the client's level of investment knowledge and to begin the educational process. Observations regarding the strengths and weaknesses of his current investment portfolio can be shared, and the client can be encouraged to begin looking at his investment portfolio in the broadest possible terms. Frequently a client initially seeks investment advice on what he should be doing with a small part of his portfolio, for example, a CD that will be maturing soon. Such a client may not realize that the decision optimally should be made within the larger context of his entire portfolio and long-term objectives. Institutional clients must likewise learn to consider investing in a wider context. For example, for a corporate defined benefit pension plan, broad thinking entails the consideration of the pension plan assets and liabilities within the larger context of the corporation as a whole. After all, it is the corporate pension plan's *sponsor* that has promised the benefit payments, not the pension plan itself. The risks and rewards of pension plan performance are therefore borne by the corporation, whose financial well-being is intimately tied to the performance of the pension plan assets.

Finally, the data-gathering session gives the adviser an excellent opportunity to communicate the investment philosophy behind the money management approach that will be used in moving the client to the realization of his investment objectives. For all of these reasons, the data-gathering session is an important step of the money management process which justifies the full involvement of both the client and adviser.

STEP 2: IDENTIFYING THE CLIENT'S NEEDS, CONSTRAINTS, AND UNIQUE CIRCUMSTANCES

Liquidity

Each client situation should be evaluated in terms of the need for portfolio liquidity. Nonliquid investments, such as direct ownership of investment real estate, should not be made if there is a likelihood that the funds will be needed to meet future expenditures. Even if there is sufficient liquidity elsewhere in the portfolio to meet such expenditures, the size of nonliquid investments must be evaluated with respect to the possible withdrawals from the portfolio. For example, assume that for a particular client, 15 percent of portfolio assets is an optimal allocation to have in nonliquid real estate investments, with the balance of the portfolio invested in a variety of liquid assets. If within a short period of time thereafter, 25 percent of the portfolio is liquidated to meet various expenditures, then the commitment to real estate will rise above the optimal 15 percent allocation to 20 percent of the portfolio. As discussed here, liquidity is an issue separate from a client's yield requirements or income needs.

Portfolio Cash Withdrawal Rate for Anticipated Expenditures

Eventually, all investment portfolios are relied on to support someone's cash needs. The timing and magnitude of required cash withdrawals from an investment portfolio should therefore be quantified and planned for in advance. With the exception of situations involving regulatory or legal yield requirements, investment portfolios generally should not be designed to intentionally produce a certain yield or income stream. The issue of portfolio design is to a large extent *independent* of the question of how to get cash out of the portfolio in order to meet necessary expenditures. As we previously discussed in detail, the balance chosen between interest-generating assets and equity assets is the primary determinant of an investment portfolio's risk/return characteristics, and this most important decision is made in reference to the portfolio's time horizon. A portfolio balanced on this basis reflects the best obtainable trade-off between the desire for stability and the need for growth. If the yield on such a properly balanced portfolio is not equivalent to what is needed for required expenditures, this is not a good reason to rebalance the portfolio toward either more or fewer interest-generating assets. Doing so causes a mismatch between the portfolio structure and time horizon with the result that the portfolio will be overexposed to either inflation or volatility, depending on the direction of rebalancing.

Provided that the rate of withdrawal from the portfolio is not unnecessarily high, most portfolios can maintain proper balance and broad diversification with more than adequate liquidity for necessary withdrawals. In practice, even passively managed portfolios need to be regularly rebalanced as capital markets move. At these rebalancing points, cash can be set aside in a money market fund and earmarked for the expenditures anticipated until the next scheduled rebalancing. This process is both simple to execute and conceptually sound from an investment management point of view.

Although it is generally true that the question of how to get money out of a portfolio should be considered independently from the determination of proper portfolio design, the two issues become intertwined where the withdrawal rate is unsustainably high relative to the size of the portfolio. For example, a client may have a 25-year time horizon over which he intends to rely on his portfolio to meet his cash needs, but is withdrawing money so quickly that the portfolio will likely be liquidated within 5 to 10 years. In this situation, the portfolio cash withdrawal rate has triggered a reduction in the investment time horizon, which in turn will influence the portfolio-balance decision. Recognize, however, that even in this situation, the portfolio-balance decision still is made with reference to the relevant investment time horizon.

Tax Situation

Some institutional clients, such as tax-qualified retirement plans, have been blessed by the tax code and provide for a tax-sheltered environment within which investments can grow. Personal clients are not so fortunate. To properly advise these clients, it is necessary to understand their tax situations. At minimum, this entails a current-year tax projection that identifies their marginal tax bracket. Preferably, the adviser will also project the client's tax situation for a few years into the future. The most obvious use of this information is in determining the advisability of utilizing federal income tax-free municipal bonds in addition to taxable corporate and government bonds in constructing the interest-generating portion of the portfolio. For example, all other things being equal, it is more advantageous for a 33 percent marginal-tax-bracket investor to own a tax-free municipal yielding 7 percent than a similar quality/maturity taxable bond with a yield of 9 percent, a third of which he loses to income taxes, leaving him with a net yield of 6 percent.

Any decision involving the possible sale of an asset needs to be evaluated with respect to its tax impact. The general rule is that investment issues take precedence over tax considerations. In other words, a client should not hold onto an unattractive investment merely because its liquidation would trigger tax liabilities. But perhaps a decision to sell an investment is made near the end of the year, and the client is expected to be in a lower marginal tax bracket the following year. In this situation, the benefit of selling later in order to save taxes needs to be weighed against the economic risk of continuing to hold the investment in the interim. These are only a few simple examples of the importance of understanding the tax dimension of a client's situation. Our current tax code is extremely complex, and there is no end to the variety and subtlety of the tax issues that can arise in the management of a client's investment portfolio. A full discussion of these issues is beyond the scope of this book. If the adviser does not have the requisite tax knowledge to handle such issues, it is wise to enlist the help of other professionals who do.

Regulatory/Legal Constraints

Constraints that are regulatory and/or legal can take a variety of forms and are more prevalent with institutional clients. For example, the Employee Retirement Income Security Act of 1974 (ERISA) governs most qualified retirement plans and contains provisions that impact the investment management process. If a client is an endowment or charitable foundation, there may be minimum distribution rules and/or yield requirements that must be adhered to. If the investment portfolio is a testamentary trust, there may be income beneficiaries who are different from the eventual inheritors of the assets. The potential adverse interests of these parties need to be considered in designing the portfolio. The trust instrument may give guidance on these issues as well as contain specific language regarding suitability standards for investments.

Personal clients encounter similar constraints with their IRAs which have detailed rules regarding contributions and withdrawals. Another example for personal clients is restricted stock that can be sold only under certain stated conditions. This list is not exhaustive, but serves to illustrate the kind of regulatory and legal constraints which need to be considered.

Time Horizon

The importance of time horizon in investment management is attested to by the fact that an entire chapter of this book has been devoted to the subject. It is the crucial variable that underlies the decision on how to allocate portfolio assets between interest-generating assets and equity assets. The two major risks confronting investment portfolios are inflation and volatility of returns. Over long time horizons, inflation is a bigger risk than market volatility. Investment portfolios with long time horizons should accordingly be more heavily weighted in equity investments to secure the long-term capital growth needed to preserve purchasing power. Over short time horizons, market volatility is more dangerous than inflation. Therefore, portfolios with short time horizons should be more heavily invested in interest-generating assets with more stable principal values.

Clients tend to underestimate their investment time horizons, with the result that portfolios tend to be overexposed to the danger of inflation, as a consequence of an underrepresentation of equities. Part of the problem is that many clients assume that their projected retirement dates define their investment time horizons. This leads to the erroneous conventional wisdom that equity investments are appropriate only while one is building net worth during the pre-retirement years. Then at retirement it is assumed such investments should be sold, with the proceeds being invested in interest-generating assets that produce the income needed in retirement. The problem with this conventional wisdom is that it ignores the fact that inflation continues to be a threat throughout the retirement years while the portfolio is being relied upon to meet necessary expenditures. For a typical husband and wife, time horizon extends until the anticipated death of the survivor of the couple. This can be quite long, and hence the need for capital growth remains. The same argument holds true for institutional portfolios, such as endowment funds or corporate qualified retirement plans, many of which expect to have perpetual existences.

Psychological and Emotional Factors

I would prefer that the investment decision-making process be a series of logical steps that systematically build to a conceptually sound, rational portfolio strategy. But, there are numerous psychological and emotional factors that can impact on this decision-making process, and it is therefore important to be aware of them. When evaluating investment alternatives, most clients have pre-existing preferences. Attempts should be made to accommodate reasonable preferences in order to maximize the client's comfort with the portfolio. But if a client's preferences are based on misconceptions or result from a lack of investment knowledge, then it is important to take the time to educate the client. Ultimately, it is the client's money and there may be limits to the extent to which a client will endorse a recommended strategy. With a good understanding of a client's psychological and emotional factors, an adviser will be better able to present new ideas in a way that facilitates their acceptance.

The Decision-making Dynamic

Institutional clients often have investment decision-making authority vested in a committee of trustees. The time horizons for these portfolios are often quite long, and trustees must assume the responsibility for making long-term investment decisions, even though their terms of office may be of limited duration. Given the many interested parties who may engage in second guessing of investment decisions, the temptation is always present for a committee of trustees to manage the money for safe short-term results. This tendency is aggravated by the practice of measuring institutional portfolio performance on a quarterly basis. Trustees need courage and confidence to do their job, and they deserve support and recognition for making tough decisions which have the potential for looking bad in the short-run, but are nevertheless wise in the long-run. By contrast, with an individual as the client, there is more continuity to decision making. The money is his own, and he can make decisions with greater flexibility and freedom.

CHAPTER 11

MANAGING CLIENT EXPECTATIONS

There is no free lunch.

—*Anonymous*

Nothing astonishes men so much as common sense and plain dealing.

—*Ralph Waldo Emerson* (1803-1882)
Art, 1841

Human wants are never satisfied.

—*J. Willard Marriott, Jr.* (1932-   )
Marriott

In this chapter we will cover Steps 3 through 5 of the Money Management Process as outlined in Figure 11-1.

STEP 3: DEVELOPING A FRAME OF REFERENCE REGARDING INVESTMENT PERFORMANCE

A sure prescription for trouble is a client who has a different "investment world view" than that of his investment adviser. For example, an investment adviser may believe it is impossible to successfully engage in market timing and therefore makes no attempt to do so. But if a client believes that it is part of the investment adviser's job to protect him from bad markets, then it is only a matter of time until ad-

FIGURE 11-1
Money Management Process

verse market conditions strain and perhaps end the advisory relationship. Clients' expectations tend to err in an optimistic direction; they believe that higher returns are possible with less risk than is actually the case. There are important advantages to both adviser and client in first managing client expectations prior to, and then throughout, the money management process. When the client and adviser share a common investment world view, they will be in agreement regarding the nature of the risks involved with, and potential rewards of, alternative strategies.

Time must be invested in educating new clients regarding the nature of the capital markets. This can be efficiently accomplished by reviewing the long-term historical performance of Treasury bills, government bonds, corporate bonds, common stocks, and inflation, as we did in Chapters 2 and 3. The simple models of security returns that we developed provide the client with a sense of comparative performance and the relative payoff for assuming various forms of risk. By gaining an appreciation of all of the types of risk confronting them, clients will understand that there is no ideal investment that is liquid with a stable principal value, and that generates returns sufficient to stay ahead of the combined impact of inflation and income taxes.

Once the myth of the ideal investment is destroyed, clients will understand the necessity of compromise in building an investment portfolio. It is possible to get stable predictable returns from some investments, but the stability is purchased at the price of lower returns. Other investments will provide the expectation of long-term growth of capital but necessarily entail the assumption of volatility. With all of the uncertainty inherent in money management, clients understandably look for some reliable constants. One constant is that people will continue to prefer stable returns over unpredictable returns. For this reason, clients can have confidence that the buying and selling activities of investors will price variable return investments like common stocks to have higher expected returns than stable principal value alternatives such as Treasury bills. Without the uncertainty and variability of common stock returns, there would be no incremental payoff for equity investing.

By guiding clients through the concept of time horizon developed in Chapter 5, you will teach them that although the passage of time does not, in equilibrium, change the expected returns of investment asset classes, it does significantly alter the magnitude of the possible penalty associated with volatility. The longer the time horizon, the more opportunities there are for good and bad years to offset one another, producing an average return that converges toward long-term expectations. Time thereby transforms the short-run enemy of volatility into a long-run friend, which fuels the higher expected return of equity investments. By cultivating realistic expectations, the foundation is laid for developing realistic investment objectives. With a proper understanding of time horizon and greater familiarity with the capital markets, a client's risk tolerance can change in the direction of being comfortable with an investment portfolio structure more well-suited to the realization of his objectives. The goal of this process is to enable the client to make an informed decision regarding how to balance the portfolio between interest-generating and equity investments. The resulting portfolio will reflect the most satisfactory compromise between the desire for stability and the need for long-term growth.

STEP 4: COMMUNICATING THE INVESTMENT PHILOSOPHY AND MONEY MANAGEMENT APPROACH

Every money management approach has an investment philosophy behind it which is built upon a particular investment world view. For example, if a money manager believes that it is possible to successfully engage in market timing, this world view will have definite implications with respect to that money manager's investment approach. Consistent with a market timer's world view is the notion that risk control and return enhancement are both achieved by continuously moving the investment portfolio from one asset class to another in order to maximize performance. In its most extreme form, this entails a policy of always concentrating 100 percent of the portfolio in the particular asset class with the highest expected return. As the expected returns for various asset classes change through time, 100 percent of the portfolio is reallocated accordingly. Risk tolerance does not need to be separately considered, because successful market timing will sidestep adverse market conditions!

The diametrically opposed world view believes that successful market timing is not possible. With this world view, risk control and return enhancement are best achieved through broad diversification among a large variety of asset classes, with the portfolio designed to match the client's risk tolerance.

Of course, there are middle ground positions between these two extremes, but they serve to illustrate the close tie between investment world view, investment philosophy, and money management approach. In my world view, asset allocation is the primary determinant of a portfolio's risk/return characteristics and is the basis for designing strategies appropriate for the realization of client objectives. This is supported by the study of the investment results of 91 large pension plans mentioned in Chapter 1. The study concluded that asset allocation explained more than 90 percent of the variance in results achieved by the pension plans. Market timing and security selection contributed surprisingly little explanatory power. If the major factors impacting portfolio performance are portfolio balance and asset allocation, then these issues deserve most of our time and energy. The art and science of portfolio management is in large measure a matter of matching the client with an appropriately diversified portfolio reflecting his capacity for tolerating risk.

STEP 5: DEVELOPING INVESTMENT OBJECTIVES AND INVESTMENT POLICIES

When a client is asked to list his financial goals, his response might be something like: "A vacation home in an exclusive resort, eight years of fully funded college and postgraduate expenses at the best private institutions for each of three children, and early retirement at age 55 with an annual income of $100,000 after taxes." With a few quick calculations, it becomes clear that to achieve these goals, a very large investment portfolio will be needed. Given reasonable capital market assumptions, most clients have portfolios that are simply too small to achieve all of their desired goals, regardless of how their portfolios are structured. Human desires tend to surpass the resources available for their fulfillment. Even if it is possible in a given situation to structure a portfolio capable of generating the return necessary to meet the objectives, it may require the assumption of an unacceptable level of portfolio volatility. For this reason, it is generally more appropriate to focus on a client's risk tolerance than return requirement. Once a client's risk tolerance is determined, the upper limit on the portfolio's long-term expected return is defined. If this return is inadequate, it is necessary for the client to prioritize his financial goals and make the necessary compromises. If the return associated with the client's maximum risk tolerance is greater than that necessary to reach his objectives, it is easy to move down the risk scale and structure a more conservative portfolio.

Chapter 6 describes the series of steps that enable an adviser to infer a client's risk tolerance, based upon the client's preferred portfolio allocation between two investment alternatives—Treasury bills and the S&P 500. The choice of broad portfolio balance is an investment policy decision that requires the active involvement of the client. Without the guidance of a skilled investment adviser, few clients are equipped to make the best choice for themselves. This is why it is so important to provide clients with a good frame of reference regarding investment performance and the importance of time horizon in money management.

The beauty of the process described in Chapter 6 is that it forces the client to acknowledge and deal realistically with the risk/return trade-off inherent in the money management process. It also fosters the formation of realistic investment performance expectations. A client generally should be encouraged to choose a portfolio balance that places him near the upper end of his risk-tolerance range, while simultaneously making sure that he can remain committed to his policy decisions through market extremes. The goal is to maximize the expected return on the portfolio subject to the client's need to sleep well at night.

Once a broad portfolio balance has been chosen, the next step is to develop a qualitative statement of the corresponding investment objective. I do not use traditional investment objectives such as "aggressive growth," "growth and current income," or "income." Rather, I prefer to word the objective in a way that acknowledges the risk/return trade-off. For example, based on my investment world view, it is impossible to have an objective of "long-term growth of capital with stability of principal value." Examples of suitable investment objectives are:

1. High total return with high portfolio volatility.
2. Moderate total return with moderate portfolio volatility.
3. Low portfolio volatility with low total return.

Once the client has chosen a portfolio reflecting his preferred balance between Treasury bills and the S&P 500, the adviser can use this information to design a portfolio with similar risk/return characteristics using three investment alternatives—Treasury bills, long-term government bonds, and the S&P 500. The addition of long-term government bonds provides for a differentiation between short-term interest-generating investments, which have little or no interest rate risk, and long-term interest-generating investments, which have high interest rate risk. These three investment alternatives serve as proxies for the broad investment classifications: short-term debt investments, long-term debt investments, and equity investments. These are the same classifications recommended in Chapter 10 for listing the client's investment assets during the data-gathering session.

The expected returns for Treasury bills and long-term government bonds can easily be found by looking up their yields to maturity in a financial publication such as *The Wall Street Journal*. According to Ibbotson Associates, the standard deviation of returns for long-term government bonds is 8.5 percent, based on the 63 years of data from 1926 through 1988. Bond returns, however, have been considerably more volatile over the recent past. For example, over the five-year period ending with 1988, long-term government bonds had a standard deviation of 13.0 percent. From the point of view of shaping client expectations, it is safer to overstate volatility than to understate it. For this reason, the higher standard deviation measurement from the more recent past is recommended. The expected return for the S&P 500 can be estimated by adding the historical equity risk premium of 6 percent (rounded to the nearest percentage) to the current Treasury bill yield. The broad portfolio allocation that forms the investment policy can now be described with the parameters shown in Table 11-1.

Once the client understands and endorses the long-term target allocation among short-term debt investments, long-term debt investments, and equity investments, these decisions should be documented in writing in the form of a statement of investment policy. Figures 11-2, 11-3, and 11-4 show examples of investment policy exhibits for lower-risk, medium-risk, and higher-risk portfolios. These statements tie together the client's objectives with the risk/return trade-off inherent in the capital markets. The investment objective is stated in a form that acknowledges this risk/return trade-off. The short-term performance benchmark is designed to give the client a simplified description of the risk/return characteristics of the portfolio. For example, the expected return of 9 percent for the lower-risk portfolio is calculated as the weighted average of the expected returns of 7 percent, 9 percent, and 13 percent, respectively, for our proxies of Treasury bills, government bonds, and the S&P 500. The long-term portfolio-balance percentage allocations are used as weights for this calculation. Similarly, a weighted average of the standard deviations of the proxies has been used in order to derive a standard deviation estimate for the portfolio.

It is always a concern that under the pressure of adverse market conditions, clients may not be able to tolerate as much risk as they thought they could at the time the asset allocation policy decisions were made. In order to maxi-

TABLE 11-1
Broad Portfolio Allocation Parameters

Investment Asset Classification	Proxy	Expected Return	Standard Deviation
Short-term debt investments	Treasury bills	7%	0%
Long-term debt investments	Govt. bonds	9	13
Equity investments	S&P 500	13	21

FIGURE 11-2
Lower-Risk Portfolio
Investment Policy Exhibit (January 1, 19XX)

Investment Objectives: Low Portfolio Volatility with Low Total Return

Long-term portfolio balance:

Short-term debt investments	55%
Long-term debt investments	15
Equity investments	30
Total investments	100%

Short-term performance benchmark*

Expected return:	9%
Typical annual range of results**	1% to 17%

* Based on a weighted average of the following expected returns and standard deviations:

	Expected return	Standard deviation
One-year Treasury bills	7%	0%
Government bonds	9%	13%
S&P 500	13%	21%

** There is a "two out of three" probability that the realized return will fall within the specified range. The volatility of the portfolio has been overstated by a "worse case" presumption of perfectly positive correlation of returns among all investments.

mize the likelihood that clients will be able to adhere to their investment policy decisions, it is better to err in the direction of understating portfolio expected returns and overstating portfolio risk. We chose Treasury bills and government bonds as proxies precisely because they were the safest and therefore the lowest yielding alternatives we could identify to represent short-term debt investments and long-term debt investments. In actuality, when the portfolio is constructed, a wide variety of investment alternatives will be utilized which together should produce an expected return in excess of that available from similar maturity government securities. For

FIGURE 11-3
Medium-Risk Portfolio
Investment Policy Exhibit (January 1, 19XX)

Investment Objectives: Moderate Total Return with Moderate
———————————— *Portfolio Volatility*

Long-term portfolio balance:

Short-term debt investments	37%
Long-term debt investments	18
Equity investments	45
Total investments	100%

Short-term performance benchmark*

Expected return: 10%
Typical annual range of results** -2% to 22%

* Based on a weighted average of the following expected returns and standard deviations:

	Expected return	Standard deviation
One-year Treasury bills	7%	0%
Government bonds	9%	13%
S&P 500	13%	21%

** There is a "two out of three" probability that the realized return will fall within the specified range. The volatility of the portfolio has been overstated by a "worse case" presumption of perfectly positive correlation of returns among all investments.

equity investments, we chose the S&P 500 as a proxy. This presumes there is no value added through superior security selection. Again, when the portfolio is constructed, a wide variety of equity alternatives will be used, which together will hopefully have an expected return at least equal to the expected return from the S&P 500. If an adviser does not have that confidence, then it is always possible to use an index fund designed to replicate the performance of the S&P 500.

FIGURE 11-4
Higher-Risk Portfolio
Investment Policy Exhibit (January 1, 19XX)

Investment Objectives: High Total Return with High Portfolio Volatility

Long-term portfolio balance:

Short-term debt investments	15%
Long-term debt investments	20
Equity investments	65
Total investments	100%

*Short-term performance benchmark**

Expected return: 11%
Typical annual range of results** -5% to 27%

* Based on a weighted average of the following expected returns and standard deviations:

	Expected return	Standard deviation
One-year Treasury bills	7%	0%
Government bonds	9%	13%
S&P 500	13%	21%

** There is a "two out of three" probability that the realized return will fall within the specified range. The volatility of the portfolio has been overstated by a "worse case" presumption of perfectly positive correlation of returns among all investments.

Based on the discussion we had in Chapter 7, we concluded that the risk of a diversified portfolio is *less than* the weighted average of the risk levels of the investments composing the portfolio. This results from the diversification effect of partially offsetting patterns of return among the investments. In these investment policy exhibits, however, the risk profiles of the portfolios are described as the weighted averages of the standard deviations of the proxies. This, in essence, describes a "worse case scenario" where all the investments in the portfolio are perfectly, positively correlated (i.e., they move together in a lockstep manner). Portfolio volatility is accordingly safely overstated.[1]

A comparison of these three asset allocation policy statements leads to several striking observations:

1. A wide variation in equity commitment has been used to differentiate the portfolios.
2. This varying equity commitment has been responsible for the wide variation of risk among the three portfolios. For example, the higher-risk portfolio has a typical range of outcomes twice as wide as that of the lower-risk portfolio.
3. Yet, for its much greater risk, the higher-risk portfolio has an expected return that is only 2 percent greater than the lower-risk portfolio.

This is simply a restatement of the risk/return trade-off discussed in detail in Chapter 6. This 2 percent incremental return would not be worth pursuing, were it not for the impact that time has on narrowing the range of outcomes coupled with the "miracle of compound interest."

An investment policy exhibit should be dated for two important reasons. First, it represents the decisions endorsed by the client at a particular point in time. These decisions may be revised in the future in the event of changes in the client's time horizon, risk tolerance, or unique needs and circumstances. Second, the capital market expected returns and standard deviations will continuously change over time, triggering the need to update the exhibit regularly.

---

[1]Based on the long-term historical cross-correlation of returns among Treasury bills, government bonds, and the S&P 500, the "typical annual range of results" on the investment policy exhibits are overstated by approximately 1.5 percent for the lower-risk portfolio to approximately 2.0 percent for the higher-risk portfolio. For example, based on long-term cross-correlations, the higher-risk portfolio's standard deviation would be approximately 2 percent less, indicating a narrower typical annual range of results of "−3 percent to 25 percent" compared with a range of "−5 percent to 27 percent" under an assumption of perfectly positive cross-correlation. Of course, an estimate of portfolio risk based on broader diversification using more asset classes would further narrow the estimated typical annual range of results.

These investment policy exhibits have been designed for conceptual and computational simplicity. They can be easily altered to incorporate additional information, such as particular portfolio constraints or unique needs and preferences of the client. For those who prefer to use a more accurate measure of the portfolio's risk/return characteristics, an asset allocation computer program can be used to estimate these numbers, based on projected expected returns, standard deviations, and cross-correlations for the various asset classes. The usual caveats apply regarding the use of asset allocation computer programs.

Congratulations! If you have guided the client successfully to this point, you have accomplished a lot. You and the client have a common frame of reference. You agree as to how and why the capital markets behave as they do. The client has developed realistic investment expectations, sound investment objectives, and a rational investment policy that describes a broad portfolio allocation consistent with his capacity to tolerate risk. Although this is a significant job, it does not require an extraordinary time commitment on the part of the client. It generally takes no more than two hours to adequately handle these tasks with a new client. Figure 11–5 is an example of an agenda that can be followed for the trustee committee meeting for a small pension plan. The meeting agenda includes a general discussion of diversification issues. The concepts developed in Chapter 7 are selectively reviewed in simplified form with the client. This helps to gain the client's confidence in the economic advantages of a broadly diversified approach. (It also serves to satisfy the client's psychological need for "bragging rights." Regardless of market conditions, a broadly diversified portfolio maximizes the likelihood that a client can point with pride to at least a portion of his portfolio!)

The pros and cons of using index funds versus professionally managed alternatives is also discussed. In determining long-term investment results, the management of asset mix dominates the management of securities within asset categories. For this reason, index funds effectively can be used as portfolio building blocks. Index funds give clients

FIGURE 11-5
ABC Pension Plan

ABC Pension Plan Trustee Committee Meeting 1

Time required for the meeting: two hours

Purpose:

To Determine the Investment Objectives, Investment Policies, Investment Performance Benchmarks, and Breadth of Diversification

Agenda:

1. Review of the Historical Performance of the Capital Markets—To provide a common frame of reference regarding investment performance and the risk/return characteristics of different types of investments.
2. Determine the Investment Objectives—Develop a qualitative statement of the goals of the money management process. The statement incorporates an acknowledgment of the risk assumed relative to the return being sought.
3. Determine the Investment Policies—Specify the long-term allocation of assets among broad investment classifications that will most effectively achieve the investment objectives determined in item 2.
4. Specify the Portfolio Risk/Return Benchmarks—Based on the investment policies, the portfolio's expected return and likely range of outcomes will be specified.
5. Diversification Issues:
    A. Decisions regarding breadth of diversification among investment asset classes. The broader the diversification, the safer the portfolio.
    B. Decisions regarding use of index funds versus professionally managed alternatives.

Documentation:

Following the meeting, the investment adviser will prepare written documentation of all the steps followed by the ABC Pension Plan Trustee Committee and the decisions reached with supporting rationale. This documentation of the investment decision-making process should be kept as a permanent record which supports fulfillment of important fiduciary responsibilities.

---

an efficient means of gaining access to various segments of the capital markets while minimizing transaction costs and management fees. The alternative to index funds is to utilize a "multiple manager" approach. To the extent to which superior managers can be identified, they can be used as specialists to add value across the wide array of capital market segments. At the same time, a multiple manager approach diversifies the portfolio among different investment styles and approaches and limits the exposure of the portfolio to the errors in judgment of any one manager.

Of course, a multimanager approach is not without its drawbacks. A group of managers acting independently can result in certain inefficiencies. For example, one manager may be buying IBM at the same time another manager is selling IBM. The results for the client are unnecessary transaction costs and a nullification of these managers' opposing judgments. In an extreme form, the use of too many managers may result in the creation of a "closet index fund" with inappropriately high transaction costs and management fees. Even if the number of managers is sufficiently controlled, a multimanager approach may create some difficulty in controlling the overall desired allocation of funds to various asset categories. Given the perceived advantages and disadvantages of both approaches, it is not surprising to find that many large institutional portfolios utilize index funds side by side with professionally managed alternatives.

CHAPTER 12

MONEY MANAGEMENT

Don't fight forces; use them.
— *R. Buckminster Fuller* (1895-1983)
Shelter, 1932

Clients love to make money and they hate to lose it. The most important conclusion of this book is that broad portfolio diversification among multiple asset categories will in the long-run deliver more return with less risk than traditional approaches that utilize fewer asset categories. Look once again at the distribution of the world's investable capital as shown in Figure 1-1. If all clients restructured their portfolios to have a meaningful allocation in each of the major asset categories shown, the risk/return characteristics of their portfolios would be substantially improved and the likelihood of their actually losing money would drop significantly.

The tendency for most money managers to underperform the market underscores the value of the performance advantages gained from a more broadly diversified approach. The remarkable aspect of this is that much of the improvement in portfolio performance flows from the simple *decision* to utilize a broader array of asset categories. This is contrasted with improvements in portfolio performance which require the exercise of superior management *skill*. Although they are more rare than most people realize, money managers with truly superior skill do exist and their contributions to improved portfolio performance can be significant. Superior skill should not, however, be relied upon as the basis for developing investment objectives and asset allocation strategies. The foundation of investment strategy

212

should be grounded in realistic capital market performance expectations. The benefits of superior skill operating within asset categories then becomes the "icing on the cake."

We will now cover steps 6 through 8 of the Money Management Process outlined in Figure 12–1. They describe a *process* for making the asset allocation decisions and selecting specific investment positions. Alternatives at each level of decision making are discussed in order to provide an overview of the issues that need to be considered. The example portfolios provide concrete illustrations of my thought process in addressing these issues. This chapter is an elucidation of this basic theme.

STEP 6: ASSET ALLOCATION AND PORTFOLIO DESIGN

Once the investment policy decisions have been made, the adviser is ready to develop a detailed allocation strategy using multiple asset categories. Figure 12–2 shows a format for progressing from the current cash value of the client's total investment portfolio to a detailed recommended portfolio structure. Starting from the left, the adviser begins by entering the current cash value of the client's total investment portfolio. Basing his recommendations on the client's investment policy decisions, the adviser enters the percentage and dollar commitment to short-term debt investments, long-term debt investments, and equity investments. Once these percentages are set, they generally remain fixed, unless there is a meaningful change in the client's risk tolerance, time horizon, or financial circumstances. Subject to the investment policy decisions, the adviser then determines an appropriate asset allocation among seven asset categories: short-term debt investments, domestic long-term debt investments, international long-term debt investments, domestic common stock investments, international common stock investments, real estate investments, and investment hedges. One approach for determining the recommended asset allocation among these asset categories is to consider their rela-

FIGURE 12-1
Money Management Process

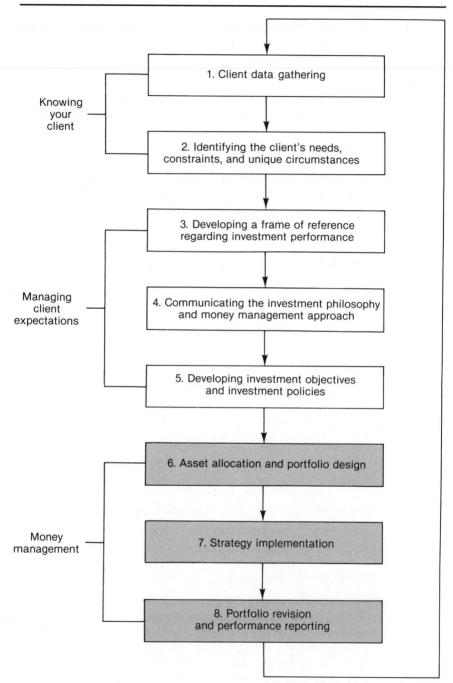

FIGURE 12–2
Investment Portfolio Design Format

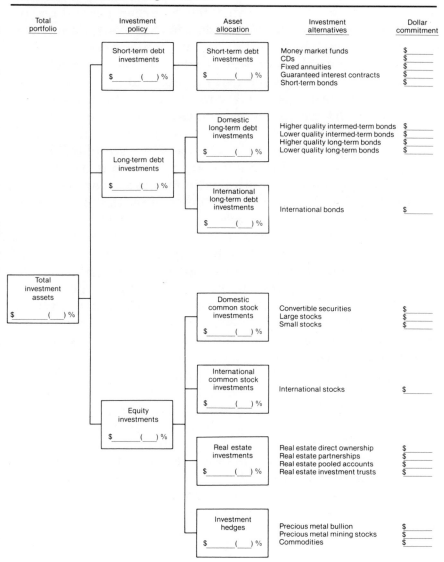

tive proportions in the world market capitalization. For example, Figure 1-1 shows that as of December 31, 1988, international bonds accounted for a larger percentage of world wealth than domestic bonds. On this basis, an adviser may decide to weight the international bonds more heavily in the portfolio than the domestic bonds. Similarly, the relative weightings of domestic versus international stocks and real estate versus other equities can be used as a basis for determining the recommended allocation. Other approaches rely on economic scenario forecasting and sophisticated projections regarding the expected returns, standard deviations, and cross-correlations among the various asset categories. Here, a computer optimization program can be useful as an additional tool to help determine the percentage commitments to the various asset categories. But because the output from such programs is quite sensitive to input variables that are very difficult to specify with confidence, computer optimization programs should be used with caution. Regardless of the approach used to determine the recommended asset allocation, it is advisable to establish minimum percentages for each of the asset categories in order to insure breadth of diversification through representation of all major investment alternatives.

A number of investment alternatives are listed beside the short-term debt investment category. The investment alternatives in this category have little or no interest rate risk. The list is not exhaustive, but provides a sample menu of possible choices. The investments are listed in the order of increasing maturity. In this manner, investments with no interest rate risk are listed first, followed by those with low interest rate risk, such as short-term bonds.

The next asset allocation category is domestic long-term debt investments. The investment choices are differentiated along two dimensions: quality and maturity. An adviser may choose to vary the allocation between intermediate-term and long-term debt based on the slope of the yield curve, or on the basis of anticipated changes in interest rates. Similarly, the allocation between high quality and low quality may be varied depending on the economic outlook.

Until more recently, international bond investing was out of reach for all but the very large investor. Fortunately, there are now a significant number of international bond mutual funds that provide an efficient low-cost means for any investor to gain access to this important diversification alternative.

Domestic common stock investments include the full range of U.S. common stock alternatives. As a hybrid investment with both debt and equity characteristics, convertible securities are classified here in order to emphasize their equity risk characteristics. (Alternatively, they could be classified under the domestic long-term debt investments category, but clients might underestimate their risk with this classification.) For simplicity, the remaining common stock investments are classified into large and small stock categories. Diversification among investment management style and approach can also be considered. At times, for example, growth managers are outperforming value managers, at other times the reverse is true. By having multiple approaches represented in the portfolio, the risk of relying on only one approach is eliminated.

International common stock investments provide an important diversification alternative to domestic stocks. This form of diversification has been more widely used than international bond diversification. Thus, the number of alternatives available to investors is correspondingly greater. Except for very large clients, the use of international stock mutual funds is preferred. Mutual funds that are composed exclusively of non-U.S. stocks can be utilized because the balance between domestic and international stocks is handled at the asset allocation level.

Real estate investments can be held in a variety of forms and several alternatives are listed. Historically, real estate investments often have had significant tax benefits. Although the Tax Reform Act of 1986 largely eliminated these benefits, it is nevertheless advisable to use real estate as an important building block for an investment portfolio. A personal residence or vacation home is usually not held primarily for investment purposes, and accordingly such homes are not listed here. Instead, they are carried on the client's balance sheet under the heading *Lifestyle assets.*

Investment hedges such as precious metals or commodities are investment positions that historically have had decidedly different patterns of return than other asset categories. The percentage commitment to them is small, and the hope is that they may perform well during adverse economic conditions when other parts of the portfolio may be losing ground. In this context, precious metals are probably the best example of an investment hedge. The investment may be in gold or silver. Less frequently, platinum is used. If precious metals are owned in physical form, bullion coins such as the one-ounce Canadian Gold Maple Leaf are preferred rather than bullion bars. Bullion coins are readily identifiable as to their gold content, and are therefore much easier to buy and sell. Precious metal mining stocks provide an alternative to physical ownership. Anyone considering mining stocks needs to decide whether to include South African mining companies in their holdings. Many of the world's most profitable gold mines are located there, but stock ownership involves obvious economic and political risks. Social issues concerning the South African government's apartheid policies will also be of major concern to many advisers and clients.

The most general level of decision making concerns investment policy. The responsibility for these decisions lies predominantly with the client. The adviser's role is to point the client in the right direction and provide the frame of reference for improving the quality of the client's decisions. As the decision-making process moves to the asset allocation level and finally to the selection of specific investment positions, the responsibility shifts predominantly to the investment adviser. The client's role at these levels becomes one of understanding and endorsing the recommendations of the investment adviser. Occasional vetoes of investment recommendations are acceptable, and may reflect the healthy involvement of the client in the money management process. But too many objections to an adviser's recommendations on asset allocation and specific investment positions reflect client resistance to the money management approach followed by the adviser. This situation is perhaps best resolved by a termination of the client-adviser relationship.

Figures 12-3, 12-4, and 12-5 show example asset allocations that correspond to the investment policy exhibits developed earlier for lower-risk, medium-risk and higher-risk portfolios. We will assume that these examples are for small institutional clients such as qualified retirement plans or endowment funds. Accordingly, preference has been given to choosing investment alternatives that are liquid and easy to value. Notice that the same building blocks are used for each portfolio. By changing the allocation of assets among short-term debt investments/long-term debt investments/equity investments, the risk profile of each portfolio is controlled at the *investment policy level*. Some investment advisers alternatively prefer to use the same asset allocation for *all* clients and accommodate differences in client risk tolerance at the level of investment position selection. For example, all clients may have 25 percent in short-term debt investments, 20 percent in long-term debt investments, and 55 percent in equity investments. But clients with lower risk tolerance will have their portfolios built with high-quality bonds, more conservative lower beta larger capitalization stocks, and unleveraged real estate, whereas clients with higher risk tolerance will have portfolios comprised of low-quality bonds, more aggressive higher beta smaller capitalization stocks, and leveraged real estate.

I prefer to handle portfolio tailoring for risk differences at the investment policy level for several reasons. First, it builds directly from the investment policy decision-making methodology described in Chapter 6. Second, it is easy for the client to understand and enhances his comfort level. Third, it facilitates the design of portfolios to accommodate investors with either unusually high or unusually low capacities for tolerating risk. Last, and most importantly, it permits a broader diversification of the portfolio for all investors regardless of risk tolerance. That is, by handling the risk tolerance issue at an investment policy level, all clients can benefit from diversification with

FIGURE 12-3
Lower-Risk Portfolio Asset Allocation (January 1, 19XX)

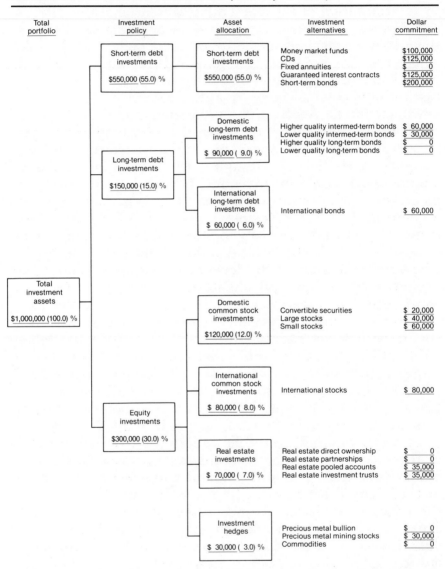

Total portfolio	Investment policy	Asset allocation	Investment alternatives	Dollar commitment
	Short-term debt investments $550,000 (55.0) %	Short-term debt investments $550,000 (55.0) %	Money market funds CDs Fixed annuities Guaranteed interest contracts Short-term bonds	$100,000 $125,000 $ 0 $125,000 $200,000
	Long-term debt investments $150,000 (15.0) %	Domestic long-term debt investments $ 90,000 (9.0) %	Higher quality intermed-term bonds Lower quality intermed-term bonds Higher quality long-term bonds Lower quality long-term bonds	$ 60,000 $ 30,000 $ 0 $ 0
		International long-term debt investments $ 60,000 (6.0) %	International bonds	$ 60,000
Total investment assets $1,000,000 (100.0) %	Equity investments $300,000 (30.0) %	Domestic common stock investments $120,000 (12.0) %	Convertible securities Large stocks Small stocks	$ 20,000 $ 40,000 $ 60,000
		International common stock investments $ 80,000 (8.0) %	International stocks	$ 80,000
		Real estate investments $ 70,000 (7.0) %	Real estate direct ownership Real estate partnerships Real estate pooled accounts Real estate investment trusts	$ 0 $ 0 $ 35,000 $ 35,000
		Investment hedges $ 30,000 (3.0) %	Precious metal bullion Precious metal mining stocks Commodities	$ 0 $ 30,000 $ 0

FIGURE 12-4
Medium-Risk Portfolio Asset Allocation (January 1, 19XX)

Total portfolio	Investment policy	Asset allocation	Investment alternatives	Dollar commitment
	Short-term debt investments $370,000 (37.0) %	Short-term debt investments $370,000 (37.0) %	Money market funds CDs Fixed annuities Guaranteed interest contracts Short-term bonds	$100,000 $ 60,000 $ 0 $ 60,000 $150,000
	Long-term debt investments $180,000 (18.0) %	Domestic long-term debt investments $108,000 (10.8) %	Higher quality intermed-term bonds Lower quality intermed-term bonds Higher quality long-term bonds Lower quality long-term bonds	$ 72,000 $ 36,000 $ 0 $ 0
		International long-term debt investments $ 72,000 (7.2) %	International bonds	$ 72,000
Total investment assets $1,000,000 (100.0) %	Equity investments $450,000 (45.0) %	Domestic common stock investments $180,000 (18.0) %	Convertible securities Large stocks Small stocks	$ 30,000 $ 60,000 $ 90,000
		International common stock investments $120,000 (12.0) %	International stocks	$120,000
		Real estate investments $100,000 (10.0) %	Real estate direct ownership Real estate partnerships Real estate pooled accounts Real estate investment trusts	$ 0 $ 0 $ 50,000 $ 50,000
		Investment hedges $ 50,000 (5.0) %	Precious metal bullion Precious metal mining stocks Commodities	$ 0 $ 50,000 $ 0

FIGURE 12-5
Higher-Risk Portfolio Asset Allocation (January 1, 19XX)

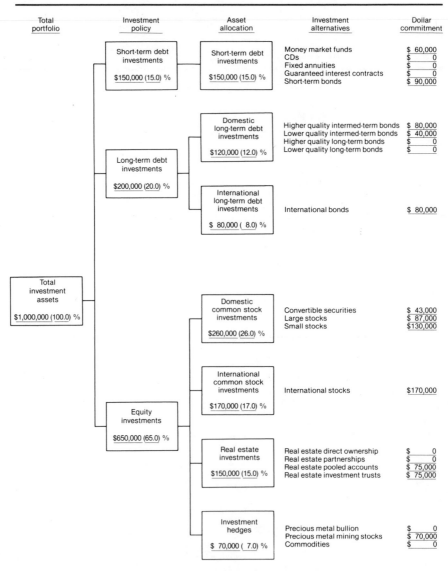

Total portfolio	Investment policy	Asset allocation	Investment alternatives	Dollar commitment
	Short-term debt investments $150,000 (15.0) %	Short-term debt investments $150,000 (15.0) %	Money market funds CDs Fixed annuities Guaranteed interest contracts Short-term bonds	$ 60,000 $ 0 $ 0 $ 0 $ 90,000
	Long-term debt investments $200,000 (20.0) %	Domestic long-term debt investments $120,000 (12.0) %	Higher quality intermed-term bonds Lower quality intermed-term bonds Higher quality long-term bonds Lower quality long-term bonds	$ 80,000 $ 40,000 $ 0 $ 0
		International long-term debt investments $ 80,000 (8.0) %	International bonds	$ 80,000
Total investment assets $1,000,000 (100.0) %	Equity investments $650,000 (65.0) %	Domestic common stock investments $260,000 (26.0) %	Convertible securities Large stocks Small stocks	$ 43,000 $ 87,000 $130,000
		International common stock investments $170,000 (17.0) %	International stocks	$170,000
		Real estate investments $150,000 (15.0) %	Real estate direct ownership Real estate partnerships Real estate pooled accounts Real estate investment trusts	$ 0 $ 0 $ 75,000 $ 75,000
		Investment hedges $ 70,000 (7.0) %	Precious metal bullion Precious metal mining stocks Commodities	$ 0 $ 70,000 $ 0

both high- and low-quality bonds, large capitalization and small capitalization stocks, high beta and low beta stocks, etc.

Occasionally, the issue is raised of using stock options and/or futures to modify the risk characteristics of a portfolio. If the need is felt to modify the risk characteristics of the portfolio, then one of two things is true. First, the portfolio allocation may have strayed from the investment policy target, and rebalancing will restore it to its appropriate risk level. The other possibility is that the investment policy is not matched to the client's risk tolerance, in which case the investment policy should be reworked. In either case, options or futures are not the preferred solution.

Figure 12–2 shows several stages of decisions making which link the investment policy decisions to the final detailed target portfolio. Each of these steps can be characterized along an active/passive dimension. Ultimately, it is the responsibility of each investment adviser to evaluate the likely gains and potential risks inherent in pursuing active strategies. For example, at the investment policy level of decision making, a passive approach requires a systematic rebalancing of the portfolio to the fixed percentage allocations that have been endorsed by the client and adviser. A more active approach would specify a range of percentage allocations for each of the three broad investment classifications. (Refer to Table 12–1.) Within these ranges, an ac-

TABLE 12–1
Medium-Risk Portfolio

Broad Investment Classification	Passive Management Fixed Percentage	Active Management Percentage Range
Short-term debt investments	37%	25–50%
Long-term debt investments	18	10–25
Equity investments	45	30–60
Total investments	100%	65% Core portfolio

tive adviser could engage in a restricted form of market timing among short-term debt investments, long-term debt investments, and equity investments. In the example shown in Table 12-1, the minimum allocations in effect guarantee that at least 65 percent of the assets will be committed to a "core portfolio" consisting of 25 percent short-term debt investments, 10 percent long-term debt investments, and 30 percent equity investments.

Figure 12-2 shows seven categories at the asset allocation level of decision making. This, too, can be handled in either an active or passive way. More active approaches presume exploitable inefficiencies among the various asset categories. By maintaining minimum and maximum percentage allocations for each asset category, the risk of errors in judgment can be kept within limits, while the attempt is made to add value. The passive alternative is to simply periodically rebalance the portfolio back to the fixed percentages established for each asset category.

When choosing investment alternatives within each of the seven asset categories, more possibilities present themselves. At one extreme, passive index funds can be used as building blocks. Alternatively, professionally managed alternatives can be used with the hope that superior security selection will add value. Other active decisions may be made, for example, in the choice of balance among quality or maturity sectors in the bond markets. For instance, long-term bonds have not been used in any of the three example portfolios shown. At first, this may appear to be a very active decision by an investment adviser who is of a relatively passive persuasion. The rationale for excluding them is based on a relatively flat yield curve at the time the example portfolio allocations were developed. That is, beyond intermediate-term maturities, there was very little incremental yield available from longer term bonds. This resulted in a situation where there was inadequate compensation for the increased interest rate risk associated with longer-maturity bonds. The only situation in which the assumption of that risk is justified, is if one is confident that interest rates will decline and wants to bet accordingly. Because the approach endorsed here is not based on forecasts of interest rate movements, it becomes a risk not worth taking. In this case, the uncertainties inherent in the capital markets argued for the exclusion of a segment of the bond market.

Another example is the choice of balance between high-quality and low-quality bonds. During good economic times, investors are often willing to hold lower-quality debt in order to obtain the higher yield. When the economy begins to falter, however, investors can become nervous about junk bonds. At such times, there is often a "flight toward quality," that negatively impacts lower-quality bonds. The benefits of diversification argue for the inclusion of both in a portfolio, but it may, nevertheless, be wise to upgrade the quality of bond holdings well in advance of a possible recession. At the time of this writing, we remain in the longest peacetime economic expansion in U.S. history. Although there is no surefire method of predicting the next recession, the duration of the current expansion makes it reasonable to assume that we must at least be in the second half of it! Accordingly, in each of the three example portfolios, money is allocated more heavily to high-quality bonds than to low-quality bonds in a ratio of two dollars to one dollar.

Two dollars are allocated to international bonds for every three dollars allocated to domestic bonds. The same ratio has been used for the allocation between international and domestic stocks. Although the size of the international commitment is high relative to the vast majority of investment portfolios, it actually represents an overcommitment to domestic securities from the point of view that U.S. stocks and bonds now account for a minority portion of the world market of stocks and bonds.

Probably the most active bet in the portfolios is the higher commitment made to small capitalization stocks. Following the stock market crash of October 1987, small stocks began to outperform large stocks for the first time in several years. Some catch up may be due for small stocks, and it is possible that this may be the beginning of a trend where small stocks may outperform large stocks.[1] While diversification is maintained in both, small companies are weighted more heavily than large companies in a ratio of three dollars to two dollars.

The relative weightings assigned to the four asset categories constituting the equity investments are relatively constant as a percentage of total equity investments across each of the three example portfolios. Because institutional client portfolios are described in the examples, real estate pooled accounts and REITS are chosen for the real estate diversification. These alternatives are easier to value and have greater liquidity—both desirable attributes for small institutional client portfolios. For similar reasons, precious metal mining stocks are utilized instead of acquiring physical ownership of precious metals.

STEP 7: STRATEGY IMPLEMENTATION

Once the blueprint for the portfolio has been developed and approved by the client, it is time to implement the strategy. If the client's current portfolio balance is different from that of the recommended target portfolio, the question arises as to the timetable for moving the portfolio to its target. For example, assume that a client currently has a short-term debt investment/long-term debt investment/equity investment portfolio balance of 70 percent/10 percent/20 percent. His target portfolio, however, is 35 percent/20 percent/45 percent. On the one hand, if his current balance is not appropriate given his objectives and risk tolerance, then there is an argument for moving the portfolio quickly to its target. On the other hand, there are offsetting economic and psychological benefits to be gained by using a dollar-cost

---

[1]Historically, the small stock premium has tended to follow a trend resulting in prolonged time periods when small stocks outperform large stocks and vice versa. This is indicated by the small stock premium's first-order autocorrelation of .38 over the 63-year period 1926 through 1988.

averaging strategy to gradually move the portfolio to its target. Dollar-cost averaging is a simple technique that requires equal dollar investments to be made in an investment at regular time intervals. For example, if we want to invest $180,000 in common stocks, this could be accomplished by investing $10,000 per month for 18 months. When placing money in investments with variable principal values, such as common stocks, ideally you want to buy when prices are low. By following a dollar-cost averaging strategy, more shares are purchased when prices are low, and fewer shares are purchased when prices are high. At the completion of the strategy, the average cost per share will be less than the average price paid for the shares. We know that in the short-run, the returns from volatile investments can be very different from average long-term expectations. By establishing an investment position with equal dollar commitments at regular intervals, the probability increases that the client's investment experience will more closely resemble longer term expectations. There are psychological advantages as well. A target portfolio may have decidedly different risk/return characteristics than a client's current portfolio. By moving to the target mix gradually, the client has a greater opportunity to become familiar with, and therefore more comfortable with, the new strategy. With greater comfort comes an increased likelihood that the client will remain committed to the strategy through good and bad market conditions.

The time frame chosen for establishing the target portfolio will be a compromise between the conflicting goals of establishing the target portfolio quickly versus taking more time to mitigate the effects of possible adverse short-run market movements. In our example, 35 percent of the client's short-term debt investments will be moved to long-term debt investments and equity investments. The more volatile the investment alternative to which you are adding money, the longer the time period during which the investments should be dollar-cost averaged. Because common stock positions are more volatile than bond positions, it may be advisable to take 12 to 24 months to move the portfolio to its target common stock commitment, but only 9 to 18 months to reach the target allocation for bonds.

Situations will arise where a client's current portfolio is already at or near the ideal allocation among short-term debt investments, long-term debt investments, and equity investments, but a different mix of investment positions is advisable. In this case, the new strategy can be implemented much more rapidly, provided the client is comfortable with the pace of implementation and appropriate consideration has been given to the tax issues involved.

Some unique planning considerations are involved with clients who have a portion of their total investment portfolio committed to tax-qualified retirement plans and IRAs.[2] We shall first consider the situation where the client has discretion over how these funds are invested. Conventional wisdom says IRAs are long-term investment vehicles. Therefore they should be funded with long-term investments, such as common stocks. As is often the case, conventional wisdom is wrong. Figure 12–6 shows a simplified example comparing the after-tax investment results achieved from alternatively funding an IRA with interest-generating investments versus equity investments. In both alternatives, the investment portfolio composition is exactly the same with identical pre-tax investment returns. The difference between the two alternatives is therefore attributable to the decision as to which investment should be made inside the IRA. To exaggerate the differences between the alternatives, it has been presumed that long-term capital gains receive favorable treatment through the exclusion from taxation of 60 percent of the gain. Without the favorable long-term capital gain tax treatment, the difference between the two outcomes would be less dramatic but would still favor the placement of interest-generating investments inside the IRA.

An IRA provides valuable tax-sheltering capability. To derive maximum advantage from this tax deferral, it is im-

---

[2]Throughout this discussion we will refer to IRAs, but the logic applies equally to tax-qualified retirement plans and other tax-deferral vehicles.

FIGURE 12-6

Comparison of Alternative Investments for Individual Retirement Accounts

Assumptions:

1. $100,000 Investment Portfolio
2. $50,000 in interest-generating investments
3. $50,000 in capital-appreciation equity investments
4. The interest-generating investments yield 10% in interest income
5. The equity investments appreciate in value 16% annually
6. The investor is in a 50% marginal tax bracket
7. The IRA account can be funded with $50,000 currently
8. At the end of a 10-year time horizon the entire Investment Portfolio will be liquidated and any additional taxes paid

ALTERNATIVE I: Fund the IRA with the Equity Investments

Inside IRA	*Outside IRA*
$ 50,000 Equity investments appreciating 16% annually for 10 years	$50,000 Interest-generating investments growing at an after-tax rate of 5% (pre-tax return is 10%) for 10 years
$220,572 Ending IRA value .50	$81,445 After-tax value of investments held outside of the IRA
$110,286 After-tax value of IRA investments if the account is liquidated	

Total after-tax value of Investment Portfolio: **$191,731**

ALTERNATIVE II: Fund the IRA with the Interest-generating Investments

Inside IRA	*Outside IRA*
$ 50,000 Interest-generating investments growing at a tax-deferred rate of 10% for 10 years	$ 50,000 Equity investments appreciating 16% annually for 10 years
	$220,572 Ending pre-tax value
	(50,000) Tax basis
$129,687 Ending IRA value .50	$170,572 Long-term capital gain
$ 64,844 After-tax value of IRA investments if the account is liquidated	.20 Effective tax rate on gain
	$ 34,114 Taxes on capital gain
	$220,572 Ending pre-tax value
	(34,114) Taxes
	$186,458 After-tax value of investments held outside of the IRA

Total after-tax value of Investment Portfolio: **$251,302**

portant to use IRAs to shelter those portfolio investments which generate the most taxable income. These are usually the lower growth, higher yielding interest-generating investments, rather than the equity investments. Please note that the logic does not work in the reverse direction. The existence of an IRA's tax-sheltering ability does not imply that they should be funded only with investments that generate high taxable income.

To facilitate the correct decision regarding IRA investments, a two-step process is recommended. First, design the target investment portfolio without regard to the fact that an IRA will shelter part of the portfolio. Second, determine which investment position in the target portfolio generates the highest taxable income per dollar invested. This is the investment that should be used inside the IRA. If there is room in the IRA for more investments, select the investment that generates the next highest taxable income from those investments remaining outside the IRA. By proceeding in this manner until the IRA is fully invested, the client will be assured of making the best use of the tax deferral available from the IRA. An added advantage associated with this process is that it helps to minimize the adverse impact of excise taxes that are levied on large retirement plan distributions. This happens because the client's tax-qualified vehicles will tend to be funded with those assets that have lower total returns.

One warning: Particularly during a strong stock market, clients may forget the rationale that resulted in the positioning of money market or bond investments inside their IRAs. Clients may ask, "Can't we find an investment for my IRA which provides a better return than a money market fund or bonds?" The adviser's answer should be, "Yes, I can find investments with better returns—common stocks, for example. Using them will make your IRA grow faster, but would also unfortunately lead to an overall lower after-tax return from the total portfolio."

Often clients do not have discretion over the investment of money in their pension and profit sharing plans. Investment advisers sometimes ignore these assets because there are no decisions to be made concerning them. This practice invites the creation of a less than optimal asset mix. Consider a client who has a $1 million investment portfolio, $400,000 of which is in an employer-sponsored retirement plan. Assume that the appropriate investment policy allocation for the client is 45 percent/15 percent/40 percent short-term debt investments/long-term debt investments/equity investments. Table 12–2(A) shows the investment portfolio balance for the $600,000 that is under the client's control, if no consideration is given to the other $400,000 in the retirement plan. Perhaps, however, the $400,000 in the employer-sponsored retirement plan is entirely invested in short-term debt investments. From the broader viewpoint of the client's entire $1 million portfolio, the actual balance is skewed heavily toward short-term debt investments, with a short-term debt investment/long-term debt investment/equity investment allocation of 67 percent/9 percent/24 percent as shown in Table 12–2(B)(1). Alternatively, if the $400,000 in the retirement plan is invested in common stocks, then the actual portfolio balance for the client is a short-term debt investment/long-term debt investment/equity investment balance of 27 percent/9 percent/64 percent as shown in Table 12–2(B)(2). Table 12–2(C) shows the required allocation of funds outside of the retirement plan in order to achieve the proper balance for the portfolio as a whole. This example underscores the importance of always making portfolio decisions from an all-inclusive point of view.

A more subtle example of the same issue involves paying careful attention to the composition of the assets *within* an employer-sponsored tax-qualified plan. It is not enough simply to make sure that the broad investment policy allocation among short-term debt investments/long-term debt investments/equity investments is correct from a total portfolio point of view. If a significant portion of the client's equity investments is inside the employer-sponsored retirement plan and heavily oriented toward large capitalization, blue-chip domestic stocks, then it may be advisable for the client to invest his personally controlled equity money heavily toward

TABLE 12-2
Portfolio Balance Where a Client Lacks Investment Discretion over a Portion of His Portfolio

Facts

$ 600,000 Fully discretionary investment funds
     400,000 Employer-sponsored retirement plan (no discretion)
$1,000,000 Total portfolio

(A) 45%/15%/40% Portfolio Balance If Considering
Only Discretionary Funds

Short-term debt investments	$270,000	45%
Long-term debt investments	90,000	15
Equity investments	240,000	40
Discretionary funds	$600,000	100%

(B) Total Portfolio Balance If (1) the Retirement Plan Is Invested
in Short-term Debt Investments

	Discretionary Funds	Retirement Plan	Total	
Short-term debt investments	$270,000	$400,000	$670,000	67%
Long-term debt investments	90,000	0	90,000	9
Equity investments	240,000	0	240,000	24
Total portfolio	$600,000	$400,000	$1,000,000	100%

Total Portfolio Balance If (2) the Retirement Plan is Invested
in Equity Investments

	Discretionary Funds	Retirement Plan	Total	
Short-term debt investments	$270,000	$ 0	$270,000	27%
Long-term debt investments	90,000	0	90,000	9
Equity investments	240,000	400,000	640,000	64
Total portfolio	$600,000	$400,000	$1,000,000	100%

(C) Required Positioning of Discretionary Funds to Maintain
Proper Portfolio Balance If (1) the Retirement Plan Is Invested
in Short-Term Debt Investments

	Discretionary Funds	Retirement Plan	Total	
Short-term debt investments	$ 50,000	$400,000	$450,000	45%
Long-term debt investments	150,000	0	150,000	15
Equity investments	400,000	0	400,000	40
Total portfolio	$600,000	$400,000	$1,000,000	100%

Table 12-2
Continued

Required Positioning of Discretionary Funds To Maintain
Proper Portfolio Balance If (2) the Retirement Plan Is Invested
in Equity Investments

	Discretionary Funds	Retirement Plan	Total	
Short-term debt investments	$450,000	$ 0	$450,000	45%
Long-term debt investments	150,000	0	150,000	15
Equity investments	0	400,000	400,000	40
Total portfolio	$600,000	$400,000	$1,000,000	100%

international stocks, real estate, and small capitalization stocks.

These issues become most pronounced in client situations that are heavily constrained. This occurred in the example in Table 12-2 where a significant percentage of the client's portfolio was under the control of the trustees of an employer-sponsored retirement plan. Similar constraints may occur where a large percentage of the client's portfolio is committed to illiquid investments. The best way to handle these situations is to nevertheless go through the exercise of developing the ideal target portfolio as if the investment process could start from an all-cash position with no constraints. A comparison between the client's current constrained portfolio and the ideal target, will immediately clarify which modifications are most important and the order in which they should be implemented. The portfolio can then be moved toward the ideal target as the constraints permit.

At times, this will lead to what may appear to be strange investment advice. Consider an extremely constrained situation where only 10 percent of a $1 million portfolio can be repositioned. Perhaps the client has at least modest diversification across all major asset categories except international bonds and precious metal investments. The adviser's recommendation may be to invest $60,000 in international bonds and $40,000 in precious metal mining stocks. Considered in isolation from the point of view of the $100,000 available for investment, this is indeed strange advice. But it is nevertheless entirely appropriate from the point of view of the total portfolio. This presents some obvious problems regarding the measurement of the investment adviser's performance results. It is thus essential that clients understand the context within which such recommendations are made. It is unlikely that any single money management organization has the investment experience and expertise needed to deliver superior results across the full range of capital market investment alternatives. To construct an investment portfolio with the breadth of diversification recommended will therefore require the utilization of multiple investment organizations.

Comprehensive portfolio management in today's world requires two separate levels of decision making. Each level can add value for the client if done properly, and each level therefore justifies appropriate compensation. The first level, which is the more important of the two, involves the development of realistic investment objectives, investment policies, and asset allocation strategies. This requires that the investment adviser have an in-depth knowledge of the client and a close working relationship with him. The second level of decision making involves the selection of individual securities within each of the many categories of investment alternatives. We have already commented on the difficulties inherent in trying to "beat the market" through superior investment skill. Those who are capable of doing so usually specialize in one particular segment of the world's capital markets, and their continued success necessitates their full-time organizational commitment to their specialty. A successful domestic small-company stock manager, for example, will most likely not become a leader in real estate investing. Similarly, managers who specialize in security selection for a particular market segment will not have the means for developing the kind of relationship needed with a client in order to tackle issues at the investment policy/asset allocation level of decision making.

The days of a client giving his investment portfolio to a single balanced manager are over. In its place is a system that requires the different skills and organizational commitments that correspond to the two levels of investment decision making described. For all but very large client accounts, mutual funds provide an excellent means of obtaining the desired breadth of diversification for an investment portfolio. This, of course, raises the issue of two layers of management fees. The two layers of fees are justified, providing that value is being added at each level of decision making. In the long-run, the investment policy and asset allocation tasks are more important with respect to their impact on long-term portfolio results than is the selection of individual issues within each investment category. These tasks accordingly deserve compensation if done well; if not done well, the adviser should be fired. Similarly, at the level of individual security selection, the money management specialist should be paid for work well-done. If a specialist does not perform adequately, a replacement should be found who will be worthy of the compensation. Alternatively, index funds can be used as portfolio building blocks.

In Chapters 10 through 12, we have completed all but the last step of the money managment process outlined in Figure 12-1. Figure 11-5 shows a sample agenda, which guides the client through the steps to determine investment objectives, investment policies, investment performance benchmarks, and the breadth of portfolio diversification. Following that meeting, the adviser develops a detailed portfolio strategy recommendation. Figure 12-7 shows an agenda for the following meeting with the client. During the second meeting, the decisions made during the first meeting are reviewed and either confirmed or modified as necessary. Then the details of the recommended strategy are discussed. Typically, the second meeting should last no more than two hours. Barring unusual complications, therefore, a client should not need to invest more than four hours of his time following the initial data gathering session in order to be knowledgeably and responsibly involved with the development of a detailed

FIGURE 12-7
ABC Pension Plan

ABC Pension Plan Trustee Committee Meeting 2

Time required for the meeting: two hours

Purpose

To Establish the Portfolio Design and the Plan for Implementation of Strategy

Agenda:

1. Review of Meeting 1—Review the written documentation of Meeting 1 and affirm the decisions made thus far. (If modification of any decision is needed, it should be made and documented before proceeding further.)
2. Professional Money Manager Selection Criteria—Discuss and review the criteria used in evaluating the universe of specialist money management organizations from which money manager selections are made.
3. Portfolio Design—Based on ABC Pension Plan's investment objectives and investment policies, discuss the specific allocation of plan assets among:
   A. Asset categories
   B. Index funds and/or professionally managed alternatives within the asset categories
4. Implementation of Strategy—Discussion of the logistics and timetable for placing investments in implementing the recommended portfolio strategy.

Documentation

Following the meeting, the investment adviser will prepare written documentation of all the steps followed by the ABC Pension Plan Trustee Committee and the decisions reached with supporting rationale. This documentation of the investment decision-making process should be kept as a permanent record that supports fulfillment of important fiduciary responsibilities.

---

investment strategy appropriate for the realization of his objectives.

STEP 8: PORTFOLIO REVISION AND PERFORMANCE REPORTING

A client's investment policy decisions define a "normal asset mix." The normal asset mix is often referred to as the *strategic asset allocation.* The normal asset mix is, by definition, the most appropriate portfolio balance to maintain on average over time, given the client's risk tolerance and investment objectives. For an adviser advocating a passive asset allocation approach, the normal asset mix is the fixed percentage allocations to be closely maintained in managing the portfolio. A passive approach presumes that markets are efficient and that gains from market timing are unlikely.

A passive approach is not synonymous with a "buy and hold" strategy. With a buy and hold strategy, there is no portfolio rebalancing. As a result, the relative proportions of short-term debt investments, long-term debt investments, and equity investments will vary over time as the capital markets move. This will produce an undesirable variation in the portfolio's risk level. In the short-run, it will also result in always being wrong at every major market turn. For example, with a buy and hold strategy, the portfolio's equity commitment and hence its risk exposure, reaches its maximum as a bull market ends and a bear market begins. Conversely, the equity commitment will be at its minimum at the end of a bear market, as the next bull market gets under way. In the long-run, a buy and hold strategy will result in a greater and greater percentage of the portfolio being committed to equities, because of their higher returns. This produces an undesirable trend of increasing risk exposure coupled with a shortening time horizon.

By contrast, a passive rebalancing of the portfolio to a target fixed percentage has several advantages.

1. It is easy to understand and implement.
2. A constant portfolio risk level is maintained for the client.
3. A balanced diversification of portfolio assets is preserved.
4. It provides a strict discipline, which prevents the portfolio from becoming overweighted in equities at market tops and underweighted in equities at market bottoms.

In order to rebalance the portfolio to the normal asset mix, money is continually reallocated from the most recent better performing investments to the relative underperformers. For example, during a bull stock market, the portfolio's equity commitment will become larger than its target allocation. Returning to the target allocation thus necessitates selling stocks during a bull market. Conversely, to maintain portfolio balance during a bear market, stocks must be bought. The passive asset allocation approach is inherently "buy low, sell high" and is also contrarian in action.

Active asset allocation can take a variety of forms. *Dynamic asset allocation* alters the asset mix in order to gain downside protection. As stock prices decline, stocks are sold, thus making the portfolio less susceptible to further losses. As stock prices advance, stocks are bought in an attempt to increase the equity participation on the upside. This approach can be characterized as "sell low, buy high."

Tactical asset allocation approaches engage in market timing in an attempt to "beat the market."[3] These approaches are buy low, sell high in their orientation. To accomplish this, deviations from the normal asset mix are intentionally made in response to perceived changing market opportunities. Of course, tactical asset allocation approaches presume the existence of exploitable market inefficiencies and the requisite skill to capitalize on them. A variety of methods are used by advisers engaged in tactical asset allocation. Many of these approaches rely on business cycle analysis involving multiple economic scenario forecasting. For example, an adviser may describe the future state of the economy according to four possibilities: depression, stagflation, favorable conditions, or high inflation. Probabilities are then assigned to each of the four possible states of the economy. To do this, projections are made for a wide variety of economic factors such as GNP growth, interest rate outlook, corporate profitability, government fiscal and monetary policy, inflation outlook, level and growth rate of pri-

---

[3]Some advisers use the term *strategic asset allocation* instead of *tactical asset allocation* to refer to the short-run alteration of asset mix in attempting to time the market.

vate versus public debt, international balance of trade, consumer spending and savings rates, currency exchange rates, etc. Next, return estimates are made for each asset category under each of the four scenarios. Finally, the expected return for each asset category is determined by taking the weighted average of each asset's return estimates for the four scenarios, using the probabilities of the scenarios as weights. Table 12–3 shows an example of these calculations. Based on a comparison of the calculated expected-returns, opportunities are hopefully identified which can be translated into advantageous deviations from the normal asset mix. To the extent to which the approach produces exploitable unique insights different from consensus market expectations, there is an opportunity to add value.

Another tactical asset allocation approach that is receiving increasing attention, involves the use of a dividend discount model to project the expected return from stocks. The approach rests on the notion that normal relationships exist between the expected returns available from cash equivalents, bonds, and common stocks. The expected return for a Treasury bill or bond is easily estimated by simply calculating the security's yield to maturity. To calculate the expected return for a stock, however, requires a different approach. For example, to calculate the expected return for IBM common stock, projections would be made of IBM's future stream of dividend payments. The expected return for IBM is simply the discount rate which equates the present value of the future stream of dividend payments to the current market value of IBM. By proceeding in this manner for all other common stocks, an expected return for the stock market as a whole can be built from the bottom up. If the spread between Treasury bill yields and the expected return on the stock market is narrow relative to normal relationships, the portfolio will be tilted toward short-term debt investments as a result of the less than normal expected payoff from owning common stocks. Conversely, if the spread is unusually wide, stocks may be undervalued and the portfolio will accordingly be tilted toward a heavier common stock commitment. Although this approach has produced

TABLE 12-3
Calculation of Expected Returns Based on Economic Scenario Forecasting

(A)	(B)	(C)	(D)	(E)	(F) = (B) × (C)	(G) = (B) × (D)	(H) = (B) × (E)
		Scenario-Based Estimated Return			Expected Return Calculation		
Economic Scenario	Probability	Treasury Bills	Bonds	Stocks	Treasury Bills	Bonds	Stocks
Depression	.1	5%	30%	−15%	.5%	3.0%	−1.5%
Stagflation	.4	9%	10%	15%	3.6	4.0	6.0
Favorable conditions	.3	7%	15%	25%	2.1	4.5	7.5
High inflation	.2	12%	−15%	12%	2.4	−3.0	2.4
Expected return =					8.6%	8.5%	14.4%

some good results in the past, as more investors utilize the approach, the efficiency of the market will increase along this dimension and the corresponding rewards from following the strategy will trend toward zero.

With less than truly superior predictive ability, it is quite easy for an active asset allocation strategy to provide returns inferior to those available with passive asset allocation approaches. For this reason, if active asset allocation strategies are employed, it is wise to establish minimum and maximum allocation limits for each asset category. This will insure some minimum level of portfolio diversification and limit the potential for problems associated with an overcommitment to a single asset category.

Performance measurement is a particularly troublesome issue for both investment advisers and their clients. One difficulty arises from the fact that the performance measurement interval, usually a calendar quarter, is much too short relative to the typical investment time horizon. The investment policy exhibit format we developed in Chapter 11 helps to overcome that problem by emphasizing that the portfolio's expected return is subject to a rather high degree of short-run uncertainty. Hopefully, this is understood when our medium-risk-tolerance client is informed with Figure 11-2 that there is a probability of two chances out of three that his return will be somewhere between −2 percent and +22 percent!

In the performance report, the portfolio's actual return can be annualized and then compared with the benchmark expected return specified on the prior investment policy exhibit. The actual returns from Treasury bills, government bonds, and the S&P 500 for the reporting period will now be known. By taking a weighted average of these three proxy realized returns, an additional comparison can be made between the hypothetical performance of a more traditionally diversified cash/bond/stock portfolio and the actual results achieved by the more broadly diversified portfolio that utilizes multiple asset categories. The expectation is that the utilization of more asset categories will produce less volatility in the portfolio returns over time. One consequence of this is the expected short-run deviation of portfolio actual returns relative to the results that would have been achieved with a similarly balanced Treasury bill/government bond/S&P 500 portfolio. For this reason, clients should not attach too much significance to whether they are ahead or behind in the short-run with a more broadly diversified strategy. The effectiveness and value of a more broadly diversified approach can only be measured over longer periods of time.

For an investment adviser pursuing an active asset allocation approach, the actual results can be compared with the results that would have been achieved had the normal asset mix been maintained. Finally, it is possible to measure returns for the various specific investment positions against appropriate benchmarks. For example, a large capitalization stock manager can have his performance measured against the S&P 500 and a high-quality bond manager's results can be compared with the Shearson Lehman Government Corporate Bond Index.

In the long-run, the goal of money management is the successful fulfillment of the client's objectives. In this context, less attention should be focused on beating the market and more attention should be given to evaluating the portfolio's performance in terms of progress being made toward the realization of the client's objectives.

CHAPTER 13

RESOLVING PROBLEMS ENCOUNTERED DURING IMPLEMENTATION

There is nothing more profitable for a man than to take good counsel with himself; for even if the event turns out contrary to one's hope, still one's decision was right, even though fortune has made it of no effect: whereas if a man acts contrary to good counsel, although by luck he gets what he had no right to expect, his decision was not any the less foolish.

—*Herodotus* (circa 485–425 B.C.)
Histories

CLIENT INERTIA

Recommendations to sell old familiar investments in order to buy new unfamiliar investments can generate client anxiety even though the changes may substantially improve the risk/return characteristics of his portfolio. This is complicated by the fact that clients tend to psychologically equate familiarity and comfort with safety. This can result in inertia. Although the recommended target portfolio looks good, it is difficult for the client to begin implementing the strategy. More than once I have had the following kind of conversation with a client:

ADVISER:

"You have a very large percentage of your total portfolio committed to XYZ stock."

CLIENT:

"Yes, it has really done well. I bought it a few years ago for 10 dollars per share, and now it is worth 85 dollars per share."

ADVISER:

"That is great performance, but I'm concerned about the diversifiable risk you retain by continuing to hold such a large position. The marketplace does not provide any compensation for risks that can be eliminated through broad diversification."

CLIENT:

"Yes, but I really like XYZ stock."

ADVISER:

"The target portfolio we have devised can accommodate a position in the stock if you prefer, but we recommend that you substantially reduce the commitment. We have considered the tax implications of our recommendation and suggest that at least one third of your position be sold this year, with another one third sold next year. The remainder can be retained."

CLIENT:

"I understand what you are saying, but why should I get off a winning horse?"

ADVISER:

"Assume for a moment that you do not own the stock, but have a sum of cash equal in value to your current stock commitment. Would you buy it today at 85 dollars per share?"

CLIENT:

"No, it's not worth 85 dollars per share!"

The conversation is followed by a long pause while the client ponders his response.

There is a tendency for clients to view appreciated assets as bargains, because they think of them in terms of their low purchase prices. Of course, historical cost has nothing to do with whether the stock will continue to perform well from its current market value of 85 dollars per share. By asking the question of whether he would purchase the stock today if he did not already own it, the client will be liberated from his preoccupation with his low historical cost. This is sometimes sufficient to resolve the issue in favor of reducing the commitment. If an inappropriately high position in the stock is retained, the client should understand that he is assuming diversifiable risk for which there is no expected compensation.

The tax issues involved with the sale of an appreciated investment often complicate the decision, however. Unless a client expects to hold the appreciated investment until he dies, the income taxes due on the gain will have to be paid sooner or later. Although it is true the taxes will not be paid until the investment is sold, the government's claim on its share of the appreciation is nevertheless there. For this reason, it may be advisable to carry the investment on the client's balance sheet at a lower value that adjusts for the anticipated taxes due upon sale. This accomplishes two things. First, it generates client awareness that the investment should not be retained merely because its sale will trigger the payment of income taxes. Second, it avoids the perception of a decrease in net worth as a result of the sale.

Another complicating factor is present when the appreciated asset has a good income yield. Although the government has a claim on the unrealized appreciation, the client nevertheless gets the entire income stream from the investment. Consider a stock with a $10 per share tax basis, now selling for $60 per share. If it pays $3.60 per year in dividends, its current income yield is 6 percent. Assume that upon sale, 30 percent of the realized gain will be lost to income taxes. This leaves after-tax sale proceeds of $45 available for repositioning. In order to generate the same $3.60 per share in income, we need to find a stock with an 8 percent yield ($45.00 $\times$ .08 = $3.60). This factor needs to be carefully weighed in the retention/disposition decision.

A client's age and health also need to be considered when evaluating the disposition of an appreciated asset. Our current income tax code provides for a "stepped-up tax basis" for appreciated assets upon the investor's death. If the investor in our previous example was terminally ill, retention of this stock would probably be advisable. Upon his death, his survivors would inherit the stock with a tax basis stepped-up to the current market value. This sidesteps the $15 that would otherwise be lost to income taxes had the stock been sold by the investor prior to his death.

Sometimes the adviser recommends that an investment be sold that has an unusually large unrealized capital loss. Here, the adviser/client conversation may sound like this:

ADVISER:

"We recommend that your position in ABC Company be liquidated because it is not a preferred investment for the recommended target portfolio we designed for you."

CLIENT:

"Yes, that stock has been rotten. I bought it for 50 dollars per share, and now it's worth only 8 dollars per share. But if I sell it now, I'll lose money."
(Note the subtle implication that if it is not sold no money is lost!)

ADVISER:

"You have already lost the money."

CLIENT:

"No I haven't, it's just a paper loss."
(The comment presumes paper losses have no economic significance.).

ADVISER:

"Assume for a moment that you do not own the stock, but have a sum of cash equal to your current commitment. Would you buy it today at 8 dollars per share?"

CLIENT:

"No way. I can't wait to sell it, and as soon as it gets back to 50 dollars per share I'm dumping it!"

The psychology underlying the "paper loss syndrome" is the conviction that no money is lost unless the position is sold, and that paper losses have no economic substance. Again, apart from tax considerations, historical cost should have nothing to do with the retention/sale decision. What the client is really resisting is the admission of having made an investment that did not work out well. Once it is sold for a loss, the verdict is unavoidably apparent. But if the investment is held, there is still hope that some day the investment will break even.

These problems can often be overcome by having the client hypothetically assume that his entire portfolio has been converted to cash before the new target portfolio is designed. This exercise frees the client from his past decisions with the result that new recommendations are no longer pitted against the sale of old and familiar positions. The entire range of investment options, including those positions the client currently owns, are available for consideration as building blocks for the target portfolio. With this approach, a client may still decide to have some of the old familiar investments retained, but the likelihood is that the chosen percentage allocation for these investments will be more reasonable.

Investment decisions should be active. Traditionally, investment recommendations have been classified as either *buy, hold,* or *sell.* I think "hold" recommendations evade the responsibility for making active decisions and that the sell rule and the buy rule should be one and the same. The general rule stated simply is: Hold in your portfolio only those investments that you would actively repurchase if you did not already own them. Sell everything else.

BIG DOLLAR DECISIONS

Investing large sums of money is an anxiety-producing situation for many clients. This is particularly true for unsophisticated clients who may have suddenly won the lottery or received a sizeable inheritance. For the first time in their lives they may be facing the need to make major investment decisions. Part of the anxiety can be alleviated by encouraging the client to think in broad terms concerning his entire portfolio and to express investment recommendations as a percentage of the total portfolio. For example, a recommendation to invest 3 percent of a $1 million portfolio in precious metals sounds much less dramatic than investing $30,000 in the same position.

RESISTANCE TO SPECIFIC INVESTMENT RECOMMENDATIONS

It is the client's money, and it is appropriate that he have veto power over any investment recommendation. Occasionally, however, a client rejects a specific investment for the wrong reasons. For example, a client may reject a recommended position in a growth stock mutual fund. As you dig deeper, it becomes apparent that he is not objecting to the specific investment recommendation. Rather, he is uncomfortable with common stocks as an asset category. When this occurs, it indicates that a prior, more general level of decision making was not properly firmed up before proceeding to the next step.

The portfolio design process should proceed top-down from the general investment policy level, to a more delineated asset allocation level, and then finally to the specific investment positions. Each level of decision making should be firmly established before you proceed to the next. If done properly, this will generate a positive momentum in the decision-making process and avoid the situation where a client objects to a specific investment for reasons that should have been handled at a more general level of decision making. It is fine for a client to object to a specific investment as long as the objection relates to that level of decision making. If it does not, it is important to withdraw the recommendation and move back to the more general level of decision making, which involves the source of the objection. The resolution may require a modification of either the investment policy decisions or asset allocation strategy, which in turn will necessitate a redesigned target portfolio.

OBTAINING CASH FROM THE PORTFOLIO FOR THE CLIENT'S EXPENDITURES

ADVISER:

"Here is the recommended target portfolio. It is broadly diversified among multiple asset categories and will maximize the expected portfolio return subject to your risk tolerance and time horizon."

CLIENT:

"Nice portfolio, but I couldn't possibly live on that yield. Why don't we cut down on the equity investments, and reposition the money in debt investments until the portfolio yield matches my income needs?"

Table 13-1 shows the components of return for three Treasury bills/S&P 500 asset mixes. Assume that a particular client should have an asset mix of 50 percent Treasury bills/50 percent S&P 500, given his investment time horizon and risk tolerance. This portfolio has an expected total return of 10 percent composed of a 5 percent current yield with a 5 percent average rate of capital appreciation. If the client has a $1 million portfolio, this mix will generate a yield of $50,000. But what if he needs $70,000 per year to live on? This would require the invasion of principal. Most clients have had it drilled into them to "never spend your principal." Although this is good advice in spirit, too literal an interpretation of the warning can result in poor investment decisions. A properly balanced portfolio maximizes the to-

TABLE 13-1
Components of Return

	Asset Mix 1	Asset Mix 2	Asset Mix 3
Treasury bills	100%	50%	0%
S&P 500	0%	50%	100%
Asset mix yield	7%	5%	3%
Capital appreciation	0	5	10
Asset mix total return	7%	10%	13%

tal return for a client subject to his risk tolerance. If the yield on the portfolio is less than what is needed for current expenditures, the client's first impulse is often to boost the portfolio yield by selling growth-oriented equity investments in order to buy more interest-generating investments. In our example, the client would have to move to a portfolio composed entirely of Treasury bills in order to generate a current income yield sufficient for his needs. Ironically, if the client does this, he will subject himself to the very danger he was trying to avoid by not spending his principal. That is, the action to increase his yield from 5 percent to 7 percent has resulted in a 3 percent reduction in total return! This increases his vulnerability to inflation, thereby subjecting the purchasing power of his portfolio to greater risk.

The solution is to educate the client to think in terms of total return (capital appreciation plus yield) rather than income yield. Within a total return framework, clients gain an appreciation that it is better to spend a little principal to supplement the lower income yield from a higher total return portfolio than to choose a portfolio with a higher income yield but lower total return.

SUSTAINABLE PORTFOLIO WITHDRAWAL RATES

In Chapter 2 we discussed the plight of a 50-year-old widow with $400,000 invested in CDs. In a world with even modest levels of persistent inflation, the purchasing power of a portfolio can significantly erode over time if too much of its average total return is used to meet expenditures. Sometimes clients respond by saying that they do not want to leave a huge portfolio to their survivors, and so periodic invasions of principal are acceptable to them. The problem with this is that even an intentional full liquidation of principal may not materially increase the cash available for meeting expenditures. For example, the widow with $400,000 invested in CDs at 8 percent has an interest income of $32,000 per year. If instead of spending only the interest, she sys-

TABLE 13-2
Sustainable Real Portfolio Withdrawal Rates

	Asset Mix 1	Asset Mix 2	Asset Mix 3
Treasury bills	100%	50%	0%
S&P 500	0%	50%	100%
Asset mix total return	7%	10%	13%
Inflation adjustment	(6)	(6)	(6)
Withdrawal rate	1%	4%	7%

tematically liquidates the principal over her 30-year life expectancy, her annual cash flow would increase by only 11 percent, to approximately $35,500. This is of little help in an inflationary environment that doubles the cost of living every 10 years.

Ideally, it would be advisable to maintain the purchasing power of the investment portfolio by limiting the portfolio withdrawals to a rate equal to the difference between the average total expected return and the average inflation rate. Table 13-2 shows the sustainable withdrawal rates for the three Treasury bills/S&P 500 asset mixes previously discussed. These withdrawal rates are obviously quite modest in relation to the size of the portfolio. But they have one important characteristic: As the portfolio maintains its purchasing power by growing at a rate sufficient to offset inflation, the cash withdrawals from the portfolio can also be increased over time to keep pace with inflation.

In practice, many clients will be unable to limit their withdrawals to the level necessary to maintain portfolio purchasing power. But if even a small portion of the total return can be left behind to partially offset inflation, the long-term financial security of the client will be enhanced.

CONCLUSION

That's enough, Charlie. Don't show me any more
figures; I've got the smell of the thing now.
> —*Henry Ford*
> To Charles Sorenson, his lieutenant

Certainty generally is illusion, and repose is not the
destiny of man.
> —*Oliver Wendell Holmes, Jr.* (1841–1935)
> The Path of the Law

The greatest gift is the power to estimate correctly
the value of things.
> —*Francois, Duc de La Rochefoucauld* (1613–1680)
> Maximes, 1664

Money management is simple, but not easy. It is simple because the principles of successful investing are relatively few
in number and are easy to understand. Although there are
a variety of risks that all clients face in the management
of their money, the two most important risks are inflation
and volatility of returns. To the extent to which a portfolio is structured to avoid one of these risks, it unfortunately
becomes exposed to the other. For this reason, clients must
determine which risk is more dangerous to them. Time horizon is the relevant dimension along which this judgment
is made. For short time horizons, volatility is a bigger risk
than inflation, and such portfolios should accordingly follow an asset allocation strategy that gives greater weight to
stable principal value interest-generating investments. For
long time horizons, inflation is the more significant danger,
and these portfolios should therefore have larger allocations
to equity investments. Regardless of the time horizon, however, the risk-mitigating benefits of broad diversification ar-

gue for the utilization of multiple asset classes for both conservative and more aggressive clients alike.

Because money management is simple, it is within the capacity of all clients to be meaningfully involved with the investment decision-making process. It is neither necessary nor advisable for a client to leave the major investment policy decisions to the sole discretion of the investment adviser. It is the client's money, and he will have to live with the results. As a client becomes better educated regarding the money management process, his risk tolerance will change toward that which is most appropriate given the facts of his situation. With greater understanding, better decisions will be made and the client will also benefit by having a realistic frame of reference for evaluating the results. This leads to greater equanimity and staying power—both of which are extremely important to the realization of investment objectives.

Although money management is simple, it is not easy. There are uncertainties inherent in the money management process which cannot be avoided, and these uncertainties are hard for clients to live with. It is natural to fear the unknown and to want to reduce or eliminate uncertainty whenever possible. But as the past Federal Reserve Chairman Paul A. Volcker said at an Institute of Chartered Financial Analysts' conference: "You cannot hedge the world."

I toured Japan many years ago. Several people in our group wanted to see majestic Mount Fuji, and so a day trip by bus was organized. We were warned before we left that there was probably no better than a 50/50 chance of actually seeing the mountain peak due to poor visibility conditions typical during that time of year. When we arrived, Mount Fuji was nowhere in sight. Heavy fog and clouds blanketed the entire valley and mountain range. Having invested four hours by bus to get there, several people decided to take pictures anyway. Despite how carefully they focused their cameras, however, the fog would not go away. All they could do was get a sharper picture of the fog. And so it is with money management. Clients often believe that as professional advisers, we should have some method to eliminate the uncertainties that are so difficult for them to live with. But as we focus on the uncertainties inherent in money management, all we can hope to accomplish is to get a better picture of the uncertainties—we cannot eliminate them. As a friend of mine who is an economist once said: "The window to the future is opaque."

As difficult as it is to live with, uncertainty is not necessarily bad. For the client with a long time horizon, short-run uncertainty is the engine that drives the higher returns of equity investing. If we can teach our clients to understand this, then they can use it to their advantage. There is a difference though between intellectually understanding something and living with the results on a day-to-day basis. Successful investing will therefore always be as much of a psychological process as it is a money management endeavor.

Money management is not easy, because without a very firm commitment to long-term investment policies within an asset allocation framework, it is easy for clients to be distracted by investment schemes that promise high returns with little or no risk. Those who depart from long-term strategy in order to pursue these investments will in the end build portfolios in the same way they collect shells at the beach—picking up whatever catches their eye at the moment. The bottom line is that no safe, quick, and easy way exists to build wealth. As an old saying reminds us: "If wishes were horses, beggars would ride."

Imagine that you are standing in the middle of a large group of one-arm bandit slot machines at a Las Vegas gambling casino. All around you, you can hear the sound of people winning as the jackpots from lucky pulls of the handle drop coins noisily into the metal catching dishes. Although it is always true that at any point in time, there are those who are ahead of the game (and these people always stand out from the crowd), on average the flow of money is from the pockets of those who play the game to the casino that owns the machines. Objectively we know this, but in the midst of the magic of a casino, excitement can override better judgment as players win just often enough to make them believe that they can get ahead by playing the game. Fueling their hope for beating this system is the evidence of their senses which tells them that other people are indeed winning—and they can, too—if only they can find a "hot" slot machine.

The messages our clients receive from the day-to-day investment environment can be as distracting and misleading as the sounds of the intermittent winnings of slot machines. Whether it is a new market timing guru or an investment idea that seems to promise better results than a well-diversified portfolio, there will always be temptations that encourage clients to depart from a well-conceived long-term strategy. At times, the adherence to long-term investment policy decisions can seem dangerous as we urge our clients during a bear market to allocate more money to common stocks in order to restore the proper balance in their portfolios. At other times, the equity commitment may become too great as a result of a market rise. To persuade clients to rebalance their portfolios back to target asset allocations in the midst of a bull market can sound like a parent telling a child that he has to leave a party just when everybody starts to really have fun. These difficulties are another reason why money management is not easy.

Historically, the money manager's job has been to enhance return and minimize risk by exercising superior skill in security selection and/or market timing. Success has been measured in terms of whether or not the manager has beaten the market. The engine driving portfolio performance was presumed to be the superior talent of the manager, and so little attention was paid to the asset allocation investment policy issues. Today, the capital markets are highly efficient and it is dangerous to presume that superior skill can be safely relied upon as the primary determinant of a portfolio's performance. If over 90 percent of future performance results will be determined by the asset allocation policies followed in the management of the portfolios, then it should be at the asset allocation investment policy level that investment advisers and their clients address issues of risk and return. This implies that investment portfolio design and performance expectations should be based primarily on the risk/return characteristics of the capital markets themselves rather than on the often elusive positive impact of active management. As R. Buckminster Fuller, creator of the Geodesic Dome said: "Use forces, don't fight them."

If money management is "simple but not easy" what are the implications of this for the investment advisory profession? Because it is simple, advisers have a tremendous opportunity to add value for clients by properly educating them. Knowledgeable clients will more likely choose and remain committed to those strategies which are most appropriate for realizing their objectives. In addition to our role as educators, we must also be architect and general contractor through the design and implementation of broadly diversified investment strategies that are built on the client's investment policy decisions. Because money management is not easy, we will continue to have important work to do on an ongoing basis. As the capital markets move, we will be needed to give perspective to our clients regarding their investment experience. Particularly during extreme market conditions, clients may need the discipline and assurance of a steady hand that urges them to remain committed to their long-term strategies. We have witnessed many changes in the world capital markets over the past several decades. More changes will undoubtedly occur in the future. In this evolving investment environment, clients do not need sporadic investment suggestions. They need, and will value, the comprehensive management of their portfolios by knowledgeable investment professionals committed to their financial well-being.

INDEX

809 648
0155

8